Gateway to UPSC Series

POLITICAL SCIENCE

Based on NCERT adaptation

For Preliminary and Main Examinations

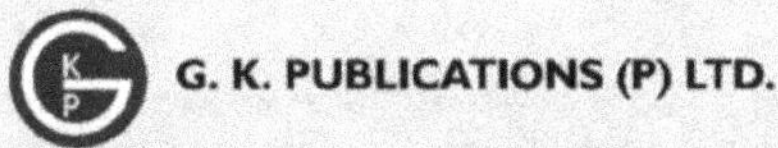

G. K. PUBLICATIONS (P) LTD.

Title	:	Gateway to UPSC Series Political Science
Language	:	English
Editor	:	Dipak Abhishek
Copyright ©	:	2023 CLIP

Typeset & Published by :

Career Launcher Infrastructure (P) Ltd.

A-45, Mohan Cooperative Industrial Area, Near Mohan Estate Metro Station, New Delhi - 110044

Marketed by :

G.K. Publications (P) Ltd.

Plot No. 9A, Sector-27A, Mathura Road, Faridabad, Haryana-121003

ISBN : **978-93-56813-35-9**

Printer's Details : Printed in India, New Delhi.

For product information :
Visit **www.gkpublications.com** or email to **gkp@gkpublications.com**

A Word to the Reader

The UPSC Civil Services is one of the most prestigious entrance examinations in our country.

The preparation spans over a long period of time and is often intense and exhausting.

The aspirant is expected to have a sound grasp on major topics such as Indian History, Indian and World Geography, Indian Economy, Indian Polity & Governance, Developments in Science and Technology especially related to India etc.

Although the qualification for appearing in the examination is an undergraduate degree, nowadays serious candidates start their preparation after completing their Class XII.

In this context, this compilation of content related to Political Science based on the NCERT aims to help the beginner to start this subject with a strong foundation. The overall content aims to deliver a clear and lucid explanation of the concepts and theories through the systematic organization and presentation of the topics.

This compilation would enable students to have a grasp on the fundamentals of the subject of Political Science. Later on, they can go for more comprehensive and focused preparation based on books by popular authors and also reputed journals and national newspapers.

We wish the beginners all the best in their endeavours.

The Publishers

Contents

1 Democracy in The Contemporary World

PHASES IN THE EXPANSION OF DEMOCRACY – THE BEGINNING

- The story of modern democracy began with the French Revolution of 1789. This popular uprising did not establish a secure and stable democracy in France. Throughout the nineteenth century, democracy in France was overthrown and restored several times. Yet the French Revolution inspired many struggles for democracy all over Europe.

When was Universal Adult Franchise Granted?	
• 1893 New Zealand	• 1917 Russia
• 1917 Russia	• 1918 Germany
• 1919 Netherlands	• 1928 Britain
• 1931 Sri Lanka	• 1934 Turkey
• 1944 France	• 1945 Japan
• 1950 India	• 1951 Argentina
• 1952 Greece	• 1955 Malaysia
• 1962 Australia	• 1965 US
• 1978 Spain	• 1994 South Africa

- In Britain, the progress towards democracy started much before the French Revolution. But the progress was very slow. Through the eighteenth and the nineteenth centuries, a series of political events reduced the power of monarchy and feudal lords. The right to vote was granted to more and more people. Around the same time as the French Revolution, the British colonies in North America declared themselves independent in 1776. In the next few years these colonies came together to form the United States of America. They adopted a democratic constitution in 1787. But here too the right to vote was limited to very few men.

- In the nineteenth century, struggles for democracy often centred round political equality, freedom and justice. One major demand was the right for every adult citizen to vote. Many European countries that were becoming more democratic did not initially allow all people to vote. In some countries, only people owning property had the right to vote. Often women did not have the right to vote. In the United States of America, the blacks all over the country could not exercise the right to vote until 1965. Those struggling for democracy wanted this right granted universally to all adults — men or women, rich or poor, white or black. This is called 'universal adult franchise' or 'universal suffrage'.

END OF COLONIALISM

- For a very long time most countries in Asia and Africa were colonies under the control of European nations. People of the colonised countries had to wage struggles to achieve independence. They not only wanted to get rid of their colonial masters, but also wished to choose their future leaders. India was one of the few colonies where people carried a nationalist struggle to liberate the country from the colonial rule. Many other countries became democracies immediately after the end of the Second World War in 1945.

- India achieved Independence in 1947 and embarked on its journey to transform itself from a subject country to a democracy. It continues to be a democracy. Most former colonies did not have such a good experience.

- The case of Ghana, a country in western Africa, illustrates the more common experience of former colonies. Ghana used to be a British colony named Gold Coast. It became independent in 1957. It was among the first countries in Africa to gain independence. It inspired other African countries to struggle for freedom. Kwame Nkrumah (pronounced Enkruma), son of a goldsmith and himself a teacher, was active in the independence struggle of his country.

- After independence, Nkrumah became the first prime minister and then the president of Ghana. Soon after, in 1966, he was overthrown by the military. Like Ghana, most countries that became democracies after gaining independence had a mixed record. They could not remain democracies for long.

RECENT PHASE

- The next big push towards democracy came after 1980, as democracy was revived in several countries of Latin America. The disintegration of the Soviet Union accelerated this process. From the story of Poland we know that the then Soviet Union controlled many of its neighboring communist countries in Eastern Europe. Poland and several other countries became free from the control of the Soviet Union during 1989-90. They chose to become democracies. Finally the Soviet Union itself broke down in 1991. The Soviet Union comprised 15 Republics. All the constituent Republics emerged as independent countries. Most of them became democracies. Thus the end of Soviet control on East Europe and the break-up of the Soviet Union led to a big change in the political map of the world.

- In this period major changes also took place in India's neighborhood. Pakistan and Bangladesh made a transition from army rule to democracy in 1990s. In Nepal, the king gave up many of his powers to become a constitutional monarch to be guided by elected leaders. However, these changes were not permanent. In 1999, General Musharraf brought back army rule in Pakistan. In 2005, the new king of Nepal dismissed the elected government and took back political freedoms that people had won in the previous decade. But, in 2008, Pakistan became democratic again and Nepal emerged as a democratic republic after abolishing the monarchy.

- Yet the overall trend in this period points to more and more countries turning to democracy. This phase still continues. By 2016, about 140 countries were holding multi-party elections. This number was higher than ever before. More than 80 previously non-democratic countries have made significant advances towards democracy since 1980. But, even today, there are many countries where people cannot express their opinion freely. They still cannot elect their leaders. They cannot take big decisions about their present and future life.

- One such country is Myanmar, previously known as Burma. It gained freedom from colonial rule in 1948 and became a democracy. But the democratic rule ended in 1962 with a military coup. In 1990, elections were held for the first time after almost 30 years. The National League for Democracy (NLD), led by Aung San Suu Kyi (pronounced Soo-chi), won the election. But the military leaders of Myanmar refused to step down and did not recognise the election results. Instead, the military put the elected pro-democracy leaders, including Suu Kyi, under house arrest. Political activists accused of even the most trivial offences have been jailed. Anyone caught publicly airing views or issuing statements critical of the regime can be sentenced up to twenty years in prison. Due to the coercive policies of the military-ruled government in Myanmar, about 6 to 10 lakh people in that country have been uprooted from their homes and have taken shelter elsewhere.

- Despite being under house arrest, Suu Kyi continued to campaign for democracy. Her struggle has won international recognition. She has also been awarded the Nobel Peace Prize. Finally, under her leadership, the NLD fought the historic 2015 elections and a democratic republic was established.

DEMOCRACY AT THE GLOBAL LEVEL

- There is no single World Government, but there are many institutions in the world that perform partially the functions of such a government. These organisations cannot command countries and citizens in a way a government can, but they do make rules that put limits on what governments can do. So, there are many institutions at the world level that perform some of the functions that a world government would perform. But we need to know just how democratic these organisations are. The yardstick here is whether each of the countries has free and equal say in the decisions that affect them. In this light let us examine the organisation of some of these world bodies.

The United Nations (UN)

- The UN is a global association of nations of the world to help cooperation in international law, security, economic development and social equity. The UN Secretary General is its chief administrative officer. The United Nations (UN) has evolved many Conventions on these questions that are now binding on most countries of the world. The UN Security Council, an organ of the UN, is responsible for maintaining peace and security among countries. It can put together an international army and take action against the wrongdoer.

- Every one of the 193 member states (as on 1 September 2012) of the UN has one vote in the UN General Assembly. It meets in regular yearly sessions under a president elected from among the representatives of the member countries. General Assembly is like the parliament where all the discussion takes place. In that sense the UN would appear to be a very democratic organisation. But the General Assembly cannot take any decision about what action should be taken in a conflict between different countries.

- The fifteen-member Security Council of the UN takes such crucial decisions. The Council has five permanent members – US, Russia, UK, France and China. Ten other members are elected by the General Assembly for two-year terms. The real power is with five permanent members. The permanent members, especially the US, contribute most of the money needed for the maintenance of the UN. Each permanent member has veto power. It means that the Council cannot take a decision if any permanent member says no to that decision. This system has led more and more people and countries to protest and demand that the UN becomes more democratic.

International Monetary Fund (IMF)

- International Monetary Fund (IMF)is one of the biggest money lenders for any country in the world. Its 189 member states (as on 12 April 2016) do not have equal voting rights. The vote of each country is weighed by how much money it has contributed to the IMF. More than 40% of the voting power in the IMF is in the hands of only seven countries (US, Japan, Germany, France, UK, Italy and Canada). The remaining 182 countries have very little say in how these international organisations take decisions.

- **The World Bank** has a similar system of voting. The President of the World Bank has always been a citizen of the US, conventionally nominated by the Treasury Secretary (Finance Minister) of the US government. However the current president is Ajay Banga and Indian born America.

- In fact, while nations are becoming more democratic than they were earlier, international organisations are becoming less democratic. Twenty years ago there were two big powers in the world: the US and the Soviet Union. The competition and conflict between these two big powers and their allies kept a certain balance in all the global organisations. After the collapse of the Soviet Union, the US appears to be the only superpower in the world. This American dominance affects the working of international organisations.

- This is not to say that there is no urge or move towards global democracy. The urge comes from people who get more opportunities to come in touch with one another. Over the last few years, the people of different countries have come together without their governments' support. They have formed global organisations against war and against domination of the world by a few countries and business companies. As in the case of democracy within the nations, the initiative for democracy among nations has come from the struggles of the people.

DEMOCRACY PROMOTION

- Recently, many powerful countries in the world, particularly the United States of America, have taken on the task of democracy promotion in the rest of the world. They say that propagating the values of democracy is not enough. Existing democracies should directly intervene in countries that are non-democratic to establish democracy there. In some cases powerful countries have launched armed attack on nondemocratic countries.

- Let us see what happened in Iraq. Iraq is a country in Western Asia. It became independent from British rule in 1932. Three decades later, there were a series of coups by military officers. Since 1968, it was ruled by Arab Socialist Ba'th Party (the Arabic word Ba'th means renaissance). Saddam Hussein, a leading Ba'th party leader, played a key role in the 1968 coup that brought the party to power. This government abolished traditional Islamic law and gave women the right to vote and several freedoms not granted in other west Asian countries. After becoming the president of Iraq in 1979, Saddam ran a dictatorial government and suppressed any dissent or opposition to his rule. He was known to have got a number of political opponents killed and persons of ethnic minorities massacred.

- The US and its allies like Britain, alleged that Iraq possessed secret nuclear weapons and other 'weapons of mass destruction' which posed a big threat to the world. But when a UN team went to Iraq to search for such weapons, it did not find any. Still the US and its allies invaded Iraq, occupied it and removed Saddam Hussein from power in 2003. The US installed an interim government of its preference. The war against Iraq was not authorised by the UN Security Council. Kofi Annan, the UN Secretary General, said that the US war on Iraq was illegal.

2 Democracy, Diversity and Discrimination

DIVERSITY IN INDIA

- India is a country of much diversity. We speak different languages, have various types of food, celebrate different festivals, and practise different religions. But actually, if you think about it, we do many things that are similar except that we do them in different ways.

- India's diversity has always been recognised as a source of its strength. When the British ruled India, women and men from different cultural, religious and regional backgrounds came together to oppose them. India's freedom movement had thousands of people of different backgrounds in it. They worked together to decide joint actions, they went to jail together, and they found different ways to oppose the British. Interestingly the British thought they could divide Indians because they were so different, and then continue to rule them. But the people showed how they could be different and yet be united in their battle against the British.

- India is both diverse and united at the same time. In the book *The Discovery of India* Jawaharlal Nehru says that Indian unity is not something imposed from the outside. It was Nehru, who coined the phrase, "unity in diversity" to describe the country.

How do we explain Diversity?

- A little more than two hundred years ago, people travelled from one part of the world to another, in ships, on horses, on camels or on foot. Often, they went in search of new lands, or new places to settle in, or for people to trade with. And because it took so long to travel, once they got to a place, people stayed there, often for a long time. Many others left their homes because there were famines and drought and they could not get enough to eat. Some went in search of work while others left because there was a war. Sometimes, as they began to make their homes in new places, people began to change a little and at other times they managed to do things in the old ways. So their languages, food, music, religions became a mix of the old and the new, and out of this intermixing of cultures, came something new and different.

- The history of many places shows us how many different cultural influences have helped to shape life and culture there. Thus regions became very diverse because of their unique histories. Similarly, diversity also comes about when people adapt their lives to the geographical area in which they live. For example, living near the sea is quite different from living in a mountainous area.

- The influence of diverse cultures is not merely a thing of the past. Our present lives are all about moving from place to place for work and with each move our cultural traditions and way of life slowly become part of the new place we are in.

Diversity and Discrimination

- Discrimination happens when people act on their prejudices or stereotypes. Prejudice means to judge other people negatively or see them as inferior. When we think that only one particular way is the best and right way to do things, we often end up not respecting others, who may prefer to do things differently.

- We can be prejudiced about many things: people's religious beliefs, the colour of their skin, the region they come from, the accent they speak in, the clothes they wear etc. Often, our prejudices about others are so strong that we don't want to form friendships with them. At times, we may even act in ways that hurt them.

- When we fix people into one image we create a stereotype. When people say that those who belong to a particular country, religion, sex, race or economic background are "stingy," "lazy," "criminal" or "dumb," they are using stereotypes. There are stingy and generous people everywhere, in every country, in every religion, in every group whether rich or poor, male or female.

- Stereotypes stop us from looking at each person as a unique individual with his or her own special qualities and skills that are different from others. They fit large numbers of people into only one pattern or type. Stereotypes affect all of us as they prevent us from doing certain things ,that we might otherwise be good at.

- Discrimination can take place because of several reasons like poverty and belonging to groups whose culture is not valued. People are engaged in different kinds of work like teaching, carpentry, pottery, weaving, fishing, farming etc. to earn a livelihood. However, certain kinds of work are valued more than others. Activities like cleaning, washing, cutting hair, picking garbage are seen as tasks that are of less value and people who do this work are seen as dirty or impure.

- Discrimination is an important aspect of the caste system. In the caste system, communities groups of people were placed in a sort of ladder where each caste was either above or below and the other. Those who placed themselves at the top of this ladder called themselves 'upper caste' and saw themselves as superior. The groups who were placed at the bottom of the ladder were seen as unworthy and called "untouchables".

- Caste rules were set which did not allow the so-called "untouchables" to take on work, other than what they were meant to do. For example, some groups were forced to pick garbage and remove dead animals from the village. But they were not allowed to enter the homes of the upper castes or take water from the village well, or even enter temples. Their children could not sit next to children of other castes in school. Thus upper castes acted in ways, which did not give the so-called "untouchables" the same rights as they enjoyed. Caste based discrimination is not only limited to preventing Dalits from undertaking certain economic activities but it also denies them the respect and dignity given to others.

- The term "Dalit" is used by people belonging to so called lower castes use to address themselves. They prefer this word to 'untouchable'. Dalit means those who have been 'broken'. This word according to Dalits, shows how social prejudices and discrimination have 'broken' the Dalit people. The government refers to this group of people as Scheduled Castes (SC).

ORIGINS OF SOCIAL DIFFERENCES

- These social differences are mostly based on accident of birth. Normally we don't choose to belong to our community. We belong to it simply because we were born into it. We all experience social differences based on accident of birth in our everyday lives. People around us are male or female, they are tall and short, have different kinds of complexions, or have different physical abilities or disabilities.

- But all kinds of social differences are not based on accident of birth. Some of the differences are based on our choices. For example, some people are atheists. They don't believe in God or any religion. Some people choose to follow a religion other than the one in which they were born. Most of us choose what to study, which occupation to take up and which games or cultural activities to take part in. All these lead to formation of social groups that are based on our choices.

- Overlapping social differences create possibilities of deep social divisions and tensions. Cross-cutting social differences are easier to accommodate. The difference between the Blacks and Whites becomes a social division in the US because the Blacks tend to be poor, homeless and discriminated against. In our country Dalits tend to be poor and landless. They often face discrimination and injustice. Consider the cases of Northern Ireland and the Netherlands. Both are predominantly Christian but divided between Catholics and Protestants. In Northern Ireland, class and religion overlap with each other. If you are Catholic, you are also more likely to be poor, and you may have suffered a history of discrimination. In the Netherlands, class and religion tend to cut across each other. Catholics and Protestants are about equally likely to be poor or rich. The result is that Catholics and Protestants have had conflicts in Northern Ireland, while they do not do so in the Netherlands.

- Social divisions of one kind or another exist in most countries. It does not matter whether the country is small or big. Even countries such as Germany and Sweden, that were once highly homogeneous, are undergoing rapid change with influx of people from other parts of the world. Migrants bring with them their own culture and tend to form a different social community. In this sense most countries of the world are multi-cultural.

POLITICS OF SOCIAL DIVISIONS

- Democracy involves competition among various political parties. Their competition tends to divide any society. If they start competing in terms of some existing social divisions, it can make social divisions into political divisions and lead to conflict, violence or even disintegration of a country. This has happened in many countries.

- Take the case of Northern Ireland. This region of the United Kingdom has been for many years the site of a violent and bitter ethno-political conflict. Its population is divided into two major sects of Christianity: 53 per cent are Protestants, while 44 per cent are Roman Catholics. The Catholics were represented by Nationalist parties who demanded that Northern Ireland be unified with the Republic of Ireland, a predominantly Catholic country. The Protestants were represented by Unionists who wanted to remain with the UK, which is predominantly protestant. Hundreds of civilians, militants and security forces were killed in the fight between Unionists and Nationalists and between the security forces of the UK and the Nationalists. It was only in 1998, that the UK government and the Nationalists reached a peace treaty after which the latter suspended their armed struggle. In Yugoslavia, the story did not have a happy ending. Political competition along religious ending ethnic lines led to the disintegration of Yugoslavia into six independent countries.

- Such examples lead some people to conclude that politics and social divisions must not be allowed to mix. But in a democracy it is only natural that political parties would talk about these divisions, make different promises to different communities, look after due representation of various communities and make policies to redress the grievances of the disadvantaged communities. Social divisions affect voting in most countries. People from one community tend to prefer some party more than others. In many countries there are parties that focus only on one community.

- At the same time, every expression of social divisions in politics does not lead to such disasters. Three factors are crucial in deciding the outcome of politics of social divisions. First of all, the outcome depends on how people perceive their identities. If people see their identities in singular and exclusive terms, it becomes very difficult to accommodate. It is much easier if the people see that their identities are multiple and are complementary with the national identity.

- Second, it depends on how political leaders raise the demands of any community. It is easier to accommodate demands that are within the constitutional framework and are not at the cost of another community.

- Third, it depends on how the government reacts to demands of different groups. If the rulers are willing to share power and accommodate the reasonable demands of minority community, social divisions become less threatening for the country. But if they try to suppress such a demand in the name of national unity, the end result is often quite the opposite. Such attempts at forced integration often sow the seeds of disintegration.

- Thus the assertion of social diversities in a country need not be seen as a source of danger. In a democracy, political expression of social divisions is very normal and can be healthy. This allows various disadvantaged and marginal social groups to express their grievances and get the government to attend to these. Expression of various kinds of social divisions in politics often results in their cancelling one another out and thus reducing their intensity. This leads to strengthening of a democracy.

FIGHT AGAINST DISCRIMINATION IN INDIA

- The struggle for freedom from British rule also included within it the struggle of large groups of people who not only fought against the British but also fought to be treated more equally. Dalits, women, tribals and peasants fought against the inequalities they experienced in their lives. Peasants and tribals fought to release themselves from the grasp of the moneylender and the high interest they were charged.

- When India became a nation in 1947, our leaders too were concerned about the different kinds of inequalities that existed. So these leaders set out a vision and goals in the Constitution to ensure that all the people of India were considered equal. This equality of all persons is seen as a key value that unites us all as Indians. Everyone has equal rights and opportunities. Untouchability is seen as a crime and has been legally abolished by law. People are free to choose the kind of work they wish to do. Government jobs are open to all people. In addition, the Constitution also placed responsibility on the government to take specific steps to realise this right to equality for poor and other such marginal communities.

- The writers of the Constitution also said that respect for diversity was a significant element in ensuring equality. They felt that people must have the freedom to follow their religion, speak their language, celebrate their festivals and express themselves freely. They said that no one language, religion or festival should become compulsory for all to follow. They said that the government must treat all religions equally. Therefore, India became a secular country where people of different religions and faiths have the freedom to practise and follow their religion without any fear of discrimination. This is seen as an important element of our unity – that we all live together and respect one other.

3 Features of Democracy

DEMOCRATIC AND NON-DEMOCRATIC GOVERNMENTS

- Democracy is a form of government in which the rulers are elected by the people. One simple factor common to all democracies: the government is chosen by the people. The above definition allows us to separate democracy from forms of government that are clearly not democratic. For example: the army rulers of Myanmar are not elected by the people. Those who happen to be in control of the army become the rulers of the country. People have no say in this decision. Dictators and monarchs are not elected by the people. The king of Saudi Arabia rule not because the people have chosen them to do so but because they happen to be born into the royal family.

- This simple definition is not adequate. It reminds us that democracy is people's rule. But if we use this definition in an unthinking manner, we would end up calling almost every government that holds an election a democracy. That would be very misleading, as every government in contemporary world wants to be called a democracy, even if it is not so. That is why we need to carefully distinguish between a government that is a democracy and one that pretends to be one. We can do so by understanding each word in this definition carefully and spelling out the features of a democratic government.

Features of Democracy

- We have started with a simple definition that democracy is a form of government in which the rulers are elected by the people.

Following are the features of democracy along with some examples:

In a democracy the final decision making power must rest with those elected by the people.

For example

- In Pakistan, General Pervez Musharraf led a military coup in October 1999. He overthrew a democratically elected government and declared himself the 'Chief Executive' of the country. Later, he changed his designation to President and in 2002 held a referendum in the country that granted him a five year extension. Pakistani media, human rights organisations and democracy activists said that the referendum was based on malpractices and fraud. In August 2002 he issued a 'Legal Framework Order' that amended the Constitution of Pakistan.

According to this Order, the President can dismiss the national and provincial assemblies. The work of the civilian cabinet is supervised by a National Security Council which is dominated by military officers. After passing this law, elections were held to the national and provincial assemblies. So Pakistan has had elections, elected representatives have some powers. But the final power rested with military officers and General Musharraf himself.

- Clearly, there are many reasons why Pakistan under General Musharraf should not be called a democracy. But let us focus on one of these. Can we say that the rulers are elected by the people in Pakistan? Not quite. People may have elected their representatives to the national and provincial assemblies but those elected representatives were not really the rulers. They cannot take the final decisions. The power to take final decision rested with army officials and with General Musharraf, and none of them were elected by the people. This happens in many dictatorships and monarchies. They formally have an elected parliament and government but the real power is with those who are not elected.

A democracy must be based on a free and fair election where those currently in power have a fair chance of losing. *For example:*

- In China, elections are regularly held after every five years for electing the country's parliament, called Quanguo Renmin Daibiao Dahui (National People's Congress). The National People's Congress has the power to appoint the President of the country. It has nearly 3,000 members elected from all over China. Some members are elected by the army. Before contesting elections, a candidate needs the approval of the Chinese Communist Party. Only those who are members of the Chinese Communist Party or eight smaller parties allied to it were allowed to contest elections held in 2002-03. The government is always formed by the Communist Party.

- Since its independence in 1930, Mexico holds elections after every six years to elect its President. The country has never been under a military or dictator's rule. But until 2000 every election was won by a party called PRI (Institutional Revolutionary Party). Opposition parties did contest elections, but never managed to win. The PRI was known to use many dirty tricks to win elections. All those who were employed in government offices had to attend its party meetings. Teachers of government schools used to force parents to vote for the PRI. Media largely ignored the activities of opposition political parties except to criticise them. Sometimes the polling booths were shifted from one place to another in the last minute, which made it difficult for people to cast their votes. The PRI spent a large sum of money in the campaign for its candidates.

- Should we consider the elections described above as examples of people electing their rulers? Reading these examples we get a sense that we cannot. There are many problems here. In China the elections do not offer the people any serious choice. They have to choose the ruling party and the candidates approved by it. Can we call this a choice? In the Mexican example, people seemed to really have a choice but in practice they had no choice. There was no way the ruling party could be defeated, even if people were against it. These are not fair elections. We can thus add a second feature to our understanding of democracy. Holding elections of any kind is not sufficient. The elections must offer a real choice between political alternatives.

In a democracy, each adult citizen must have one vote and each vote must have one value, because democracy is based on a fundamental principle of political equality.

Some of the contrary examples are:

- Until 2015, in Saudi Arabia women did not have the right to vote.

- Estonia has made its citizenship rules in such a way that people belonging to Russian minority find it difficult to get the right to vote.

- In Fiji, the electoral system is such that the vote of an indigenous Fiji has more value than that of an Indian-Fijian.

A democratic government rules within limits set by constitutional law and citizens' rights.
For example:

- Zimbabwe attained independence from White minority rule in 1980. Since then the country has been ruled by ZANU-PF, the party that led the freedom struggle. Its leader, Robert Mugabe, ruled the country since independence. Elections were held regularly and always won by ZANU-PF. President Mugabe was popular but also used unfair practices in elections. Over the years, his government changed the constitution several times to increase the powers of the President and make him less accountable. Opposition party workers were harassed and their meeting disrupted. Public protests and demonstrations against the government were declared illegal. There was a law that limited the right to criticise the President. Television and radio were controlled by the government and gave only the ruling party's version. There were independent newspapers but the government harassed those journalists who went against it. The government ignored some court judgments that went against it and pressurised judges. He was forced out of office in 2017.

- The example of Zimbabwe shows that popular approval of the rulers is necessary in a democracy, but it is not sufficient. Popular governments can be undemocratic. Popular leaders can be autocratic. If we wish to assess a democracy, it is important to look at the elections. But it is equally important to look before and after the elections. There should be sufficient room for normal political activity, including political opposition, in the period before elections. This requires that the state should respect some basic rights of the citizen. They should be free to think, to have opinions, to express these in public, to form associations, to protest and take other political actions. Everyone should be equal in the eyes of law. These rights must be protected by an independent judiciary whose orders are obeyed by everyone.

Hence, democracy is a form of government in which:

- Rulers elected by the people take all the major decisions;
- Elections offer a choice and fair opportunity to the people to change the current rulers;
- This choice and opportunity is available to all the people on an equal basis; and
- The exercise of this choice leads to a government limited by basic rules of the constitution and citizens' rights.

4 Democratic Governments

INTRODUCTION

- Democratic governments in our times are usually referred to as representative democracies. In representative democracies people do not participate directly but, instead, choose their representatives through an election process. These representatives meet and make decisions for the entire population. These days, a government cannot call itself democratic unless it allows what is known as universal adult franchise. This means that all adults in the country are allowed to vote.

- But there was a time when governments did not allow women and the poor to participate in elections. In their earliest forms governments allowed only men who owned property and were educated, to vote. This meant that women, the poor, the property-less and the uneducated were not allowed to vote.

- In India, before Independence, only a small minority was allowed to vote and they therefore came together to determine the fate of the majority. Several people including Gandhiji were shocked at the unfairness of this practice and demanded that all adults have the right to vote. This is known as universal adult franchise.

- Writing in the journal *Young India* in 1931, Gandhiji said, "I cannot possibly bear the idea that a man who has got wealth should have the vote, but that a man who has got character but no wealth or literacy should have no vote, or that a man who works honestly by the sweat of his brow day in and day out should not have the vote for the crime of being a poor man...".

RIGHTS IN A DEMOCRACY

- Rights are reasonable claims of persons recognised by society and sanctioned by law. A right is possible when you make a claim that is equally possible for others. Rights are necessary for the very sustenance of a democracy. In a democracy every citizen has to have the right to vote and the right to be elected to government. For democratic elections to take place, it is necessary that citizens should have the right to express their opinion, form political parties and take part in political activities.

- Rights also perform a very special role in a democracy. Rights protect minorities from the oppression of majority. They ensure that the majority cannot do whatever it likes. Rights are guarantees which can be used when things go wrong. Things may go wrong when some citizens may wish to take away the rights of others. This usually happens when those in majority want to dominate those in minority. The government should protect the citizens' rights in such a situation. But sometimes elected governments may not protect or may even attack the rights of their own citizens. That is why some rights need to be placed higher than the government, so that the government cannot violate them. In most democracies the basic rights of the citizen are written down in the constitution.

ELECTION IN A DEMOCRACY

- Elections take place regularly in any democracy. There are more than one hundred countries in the world in which elections take place to choose people's representatives. Also elections are held in many countries that are not democratic.

- But why do we need elections? Let us try to imagine a democracy without elections. A rule of the people is possible without any elections if all the people can sit together every day and take all the decisions. But this is not possible in any large community. Nor is it possible for everyone to have the time and knowledge to take decisions on all matters. Therefore in most democracies people rule through their representatives. In an election the voters make many choices:

- They can choose who will make laws for them.

- They can choose who will form the government and take major decisions.

- They can choose the party whose policies will guide the government and law making.

Elections can be held in many ways. All democratic countries hold elections. But most non-democratic countries also hold some kind of elections. We have seen examples above to distinguish democratic elections from any other election. *A list of some conditions of a democratic election are:*

- First, everyone should be able to choose. This means that everyone should have one vote and every vote should have equal value.

- Second, there should be something to choose from. Parties and candidates should be free to contest elections and should offer some real choice to the voters.

- Third, the choice should be offered at regular intervals. Elections must be held regularly after every few years.

- Fourth, the candidate preferred by the people should get elected.

- Fifth, elections should be conducted in a free and fair manner where people can choose as they really wish.

PARTICIPATION IN A DEMOCRACY

- Through voting in elections people elect leaders to represent them. These representatives take decisions on behalf of the people. In doing so it is assumed that they will keep in mind the voices and interests of the people.

- All governments are elected for fixed periods. In India this period is five years. Once elected, governments can stay in power only for that period. If they want to continue to be in power then they have to be re-elected by the people. This is a moment when people can sense their power in a democracy. In this way the power of the government gets limited by regular elections.

- Besides voting there are other ways of participating in the process of. People participate by taking an interest in the working of the government and by criticising it when required. There are many ways in which people express their views and make governments understand what actions they should take. These include dharnas, rallies, strikes, signature campaigns etc. Things that are unfair and unjust are also brought forward. Newspapers, magazines and TV also play a role in discussing government issues and responsibilities.

POLITICAL COMPETITION IN A DEMOCRACY

- Elections are thus all about political competition. This competition takes various forms. The most obvious form is the competition among political parties. At the constituency level, it takes the form of competition among several candidates. If there is no competition, elections will become pointless.

- An electoral competition has many demerits. It creates a sense of disunity and 'factionalism' in every locality. You would have heard of people complaining of 'party-politics' in your locality. Different political parties and leaders often level allegations against one another. Parties and candidates often use dirty tricks to win elections. Some people say that this pressure to win electoral fights does not allow sensible long-term policies to be formulated. Some good people who may wish to serve the country do not enter this arena. They do not like the idea of being dragged into unhealthy competition.

- Our Constitution makers were aware of these problems. Yet they opted for free competition in elections as the way to select our future leaders. They did so because this system works better in the long run. This is because political leaders all over the world, like all other professionals, are motivated by a desire to advance their political careers. They want to remain in power or get power and positions for themselves. They may wish to serve the people as well, but it is risky to depend entirely on their sense of duty. Besides, even when they wish to serve the people, they may not know what is required to do so, or their ideas may not match what the people really want.

- So the realistic solution to this problem is to set up a system where political leaders are rewarded for serving the people and punished for not doing so. Regular electoral competition provides incentives to political parties and leaders. They know that if they raise issues that people want to be raised, their popularity and chances of victory will increase in the next elections. But if they fail to satisfy the voters with their work they will not be able to win again. So if a political party is motivated only by desire to be in power, even then it will be forced to serve the people.

ARGUMENTS AGAINST DEMOCRACY

- Democracy is not a magical solution for all the problems. It has not ended poverty in our country and in other parts of the world. Democracy as a form of government only ensures that people take their own decisions. This does not guarantee that their decisions will be good. People can make mistakes. Involving the people in these decisions does lead to delays in decision making. Sometimes this can set back big decisions and affect the government's efficiency.

Some of the other arguments against democracy are:

- Leaders keep changing in a democracy. This leads to instability.
- Democracy is all about political competition and power play. There is no scope for morality.
- So many people have to be consulted in a democracy that it leads to delays.
- Elected leaders do not know the best interest of the people. It leads to bad decisions.
- Democracy leads to corruption for it is based on electoral competition.
- Ordinary people don't know what is good for them.

Some of the other arguments for democracy are:

- A democratic government is a better government because it is a more accountable form of government.
- Democracy is based on consultation and discussion. A democratic decision always involves many persons, discussions and meetings. Thus democracy improves the quality of decision-making.
- Democracy provides a method to deal with differences and conflicts. In any society people are bound to have differences of opinions and interests. These differences are particularly sharp in a country like ours which has an amazing social and linguistic diversity. Different groups can live with one another peacefully. In a diverse country like India, democracy keeps our country together.
- Democracy enhances the dignity of citizens. As democracy is based on the principle of political equality, on recognising that the poorest and the least educated has the same status as the rich and the educated. People are not subjects of a ruler, they are the rulers themselves. Even when they make mistakes, they are responsible for their conduct.
- Finally, democracy is better than other forms of government because it allows us to correct its own mistakes. There is always a room for correction. Either the rulers have to change their decisions, or the rulers can be changed. This cannot happen in a non-democratic government.
- Democracy cannot get us everything and is not the solution to all problems. But it is clearly better than any other alternative that we know and considered as the best form of government.

Do You Know?

- American women got the right to vote in 1920 while women in the UK got to vote on the same terms as men some years later, in 1928.
- South Africa was earlier governed by apartheid laws. Apartheid means separation on the basis of race. South African people were divided into white, black, Indian and coloured races. According to the law, these races were not allowed to mingle with each other, to live near each other or even to use common facilities. The African National Congress, a group of people who led the struggle against apartheid, and their most well-known leader, Nelson Mandela fought the apartheid system for several years. Finally, they succeeded, and in 1994 South Africa became a democratic country in which people of all races were considered equal.

- The Government of India had appointed the Second Backward Classes Commission in 1979. It was headed by B.P. Mandal. Hence it was popularly called the Mandal Commission. It was asked to determine the criteria to identify the socially and educationally backward classes in India and recommend steps to be taken for their advancement. The Commission gave its Report in 1980 and made many recommendations. One of these was that 27 per cent of government jobs be reserved for the socially and educationally backward classes. The Report and recommendations were discussed in the Parliament.

- On 6 August 1990, the Union Cabinet took a formal decision to implement the recommendations. Next day Prime Minister V.P. Singh informed the Parliament about this decision through a statement in both the Houses of Parliament.

- In 'Indira Sawhney and others Vs Union of India case', Eleven judges of the Supreme Court heard arguments of both sides. By a majority, the Supreme Court judges in 1992 declared that this order of the Government of India was valid. At the same time the Supreme Court asked the government to modify its original order. It said that well-todo persons among the backward classes should be excluded from getting the benefit of reservation.

5 Understanding Marginalisation

MINORITIES AND MARGINALISATION

- The term minority is most commonly used to refer to communities that are numerically small in relation to the rest of the population. However, it is a concept that goes well beyond numbers. It encompasses issues of power, access to resources and has social and cultural dimensions. The Indian Constitution recognised that the culture of the majority influences the way in which society and government might express themselves. In such cases, size can be a disadvantage and lead to the marginalisation of the relatively smaller communities. Thus, safeguards are needed to protect minority communities against the possibility of being culturally dominated by the majority. They also protect them against any discrimination and disadvantage that they may face. Given certain conditions, communities that are small in number relative to the rest of society may feel insecure about their lives, assets and well-being. This sense of insecurity may get accentuated if the relations between the minority and majority communities are fraught. The Constitution provides these safeguards because it is committed to protecting India's cultural diversity and promoting equality as well as justice. The judiciary plays a crucial role in upholding the law and enforcing Fundamental Rights. Every citizen of India can approach the courts if they believe that their Fundamental Rights have been violated. Now let us understand marginalisation in the context of the Muslim community.

MUSLIMS AND MARGINALISATION

- According to 2011 census, Muslims are 14.2 per cent of India's population and are considered to be a marginalised community in India today because in comparison to other communities, they have over the years been deprived of the benefits of socioeconomic development.

- Recognising that Muslims in India were lagging behind in terms of various development indicators, the government set up a high-level committee in 2005. Chaired by Justice Rajindar Sachar, the committee examined the social, economic and educational status of the Muslim community in India. The report discusses in detail the marginalisation of this community. It suggests that on a range of social, economic and educational indicators the situation of the Muslim community is comparable to that of other marginalised communities like Scheduled Castes and Scheduled Tribes.

- Economic and social marginalisation experienced by Muslims has other dimensions as well. Like other minorities, Muslim customs and practices are sometimes quite distinct from what is seen as the mainstream. Some –not all – Muslims may wear a burqa, sport a long beard, wear a fez, and these become ways to identify all Muslims. Because of this, they tend to be identified differently and some people think they are not like the 'rest of us'. Often this becomes an excuse to treat them unfairly, and discriminate against them. This social marginalisation of Muslims in some instances has led to them migrating from places where they have lived, often leading to the ghettoisation of the community. Sometimes, this prejudice leads to hatred and violence.

WHO ARE ADIVASIS?

- Adivasis – the term literally means 'original inhabitants'– are communities who lived, and often continue to live, in close association with forests. Around 8 per cent of India's population is Adivasi and many of India's most important mining and industrial centres are located in Adivasi areas – Jamshedpur, Rourkela, Bokaro and Bhilai among others. Adivasis are not a homogeneous population: there are over 500 different Adivasi groups in India. Adivasis are particularly numerous in states like Chhattisgarh, Jharkhand, Madhya Pradesh, Orissa, Gujarat, Maharashtra, Rajasthan, Andhra Pradesh, West Bengal and in the north-eastern states of Arunachal Pradesh, Assam, Manipur, Meghalaya, Mizoram, Nagaland and Tripura. A state like Orissa is home to more than 60 different tribal groups. Adivasi societies are also most distinctive because there is often very little hierarchy among them. This makes them radically different from communities organised around principles of jati-varna (caste) or those that were ruled by kings.

- Adivasis practise a range of tribal religions that are different from Islam, Hinduism and Christianity. These often involve the worship of ancestors, village and nature spirits, the last associated with and residing in various sites in the landscape – 'mountain-spirits', 'river-spirits', 'animal-spirits', etc. The village spirits are often worshipped at specific sacred groves within the village boundary while the ancestral ones are usually worshipped at home. Additionally, Adivasis have always been influenced by different surrounding religions like Shakta, Buddhist, Vaishnav, Bhakti and Christianity. Simultaneously, Adivasi religions themselves have influenced dominant religions of the empires around them, for example, the Jagannath cult of Orissa and Shakti and Tantric traditions in Bengal and Assam. During the nineteenth century, substantial numbers of Adivasis converted to Christianity, which has emerged as a very important religion in modern Adivasi history. Adivasis have their own languages (most of them radically different from and possibly as old as Sanskrit), which have often deeply influenced the formation of 'mainstream' Indian languages, like Bengali. Santhali has the largest number of speakers and has a significant body of publications including magazines on the internet or in e-zines.

Adivasis and Stereotyping

- In India, we usually 'showcase' Adivasi communities in particular ways. Thus, during school functions or other official events or in books and movies, Adivasis are invariably portrayed in very stereotypical ways – in colourful costumes, headgear and through their dancing. Besides this, we seem to know very little about the realities of their lives. This often wrongly leads to people believing that they are exotic, primitive and backward. Often Adivasis are blamed for their lack of advancement as they are believed to be resistant to change or new ideas.

Adivasis and Development

- Metal ores like iron and copper, and gold and silver, coal and diamonds, invaluable timber, most medicinal herbs and animal products (wax, lac, honey) and animals themselves (elephants, the mainstay of imperial armies), all came from the forests. In addition, the continuation of life depended heavily on forests, that help recharge many of India's rivers and, as is becoming clearer now, crucial to the availability and quality of our air and water. Forests covered the major part of our country till the nineteenth century and the Adivasis had a deep knowledge of, access to, as well as control over most of these vast tracts at least till the middle of the nineteenth century. This meant that they were not ruled by large states and empires. Instead, often empires heavily depended on Adivasis for the crucial access to forest resources.

- This is radically contrary to our image of Adivasis today as somewhat marginal and powerless communities. In the pre-colonial world, they were traditionally ranged hunter gatherers and nomads and lived by shifting agriculture and also cultivating in one place. Although these remain, for the past 200 years Adivasis have been increasingly forced –through economic changes, forest policies and political force applied by the State and private industry – to migrate to lives as workers in plantations, at construction sites, in industries and as domestic workers. For the first time in history, they do not control or have much direct access to the forest territories.

- Forest lands have been cleared for timber and to get land for agriculture and industry. Adivasis have also lived in areas that are rich in minerals and other natural resources. These are taken over for mining and other large industrial projects. Powerful forces have often colluded to take over tribal land. Much of the time, the land is taken away forcefully and procedures are not followed. According to official figures, more than 50 per cent of persons displaced due to mines and mining projects are tribals. Another recent survey report by organisations working among Adivasis shows that 79 per cent of the persons displaced from the states of Andhra Pradesh, Chhattisgarh, Orissa and Jharkhand are tribals. Huge tracts of their lands have also gone under the waters of hundreds of dams that have been built in independent India. In the North east, their lands remain highly militarised and war-torn. India has 54 national parks and 372 wildlife sanctuaries covering 1,09,652 sq km. These are areas where tribals originally lived but were evicted from. When they continue to stay in these forests, they are termed encroachers. Losing their lands and access to the forest means that tribal lose their main sources of livelihood and food. Having gradually lost access to their traditional homelands, many Adivasis have migrated to cities in search of work where they are employed for very low wages in local industries or at building or construction sites. They, thus, get caught in a cycle of poverty and deprivation. 45 per cent of tribal groups in rural areas and 35 per cent in urban areas live below the poverty line. This leads to deprivation in other areas. Many tribal children are malnourished. Literacy rates among tribal are also very low. When Adivasis are displaced from their lands, they lose much more than a source of income. They lose their traditions and customs – a way of living and being. "They took our farming land. They left some houses. They took the cremation ground, temple, well and pond. How will we survive?" says Gobindha Maran, who was displaced due to a refinery project in Orissa.

CONFRONTING MARGINALISATION – INVOKING FUNDAMENTAL RIGHTS

- As far as the marginalised are concerned, they have drawn on these rights in two ways: first, by insisting on their Fundamental Rights, they have forced the government to recognise the injustice done to them. Second, they have insisted that the government enforce these laws. In some instances, the struggles of the marginalised have influenced the government to frame new laws, in keeping with the spirit of the Fundamental Rights.

- Article 17 of the Constitution states that untouchability has been abolished – what this means is that no one can henceforth prevent Dalits from educating themselves, entering temples, using public facilities etc. It also means that it is wrong to practise untouchability and that this practice will not be tolerated by a democratic government. In fact, untouchability is a punishable crime now.

- There are other sections in the Constitution that help to strengthen the argument against untouchability – for example, Article 15 of the Constitution notes that no citizen of India shall be discriminated against on the basis of religion, race, caste, sex or place of birth. This has been used by Dalits to seek equality where it has been denied to them.

- Likewise, other minority groups have drawn on the Fundamental Rights section of our Constitution. They have particularly drawn upon the right to freedom of religion and cultural and educational rights. In the case of cultural and educational rights, distinct cultural and religious groups like the Muslims and Parsis have the right to be the guardians of the content of their culture, as well as the right to make decisions on how best this content is to be preserved. Thus, by granting different forms of cultural rights, the Constitution tries to ensure cultural justice to such groups. The Constitution does this so that the culture of these groups is not dominated nor wiped out by the culture of the majority community.

LAWS FOR THE MARGINALISED

- There are specific laws and policies for the marginalised in our country. There are policies or schemes that emerge through other means like setting up a committee or by undertaking a survey etc. The government then makes an effort to promote such policies in order to give opportunities to specific groups.

PROMOTING SOCIAL JUSTICE

- As part of their effort to implement the Constitution, both state and central governments create specific schemes for implementation in tribal areas or in areas that have a high Dalit population. For example, the government provides for free or subsidised hostels for students of Dalit and Adivasi communities so that they can avail of education facilities that may not be available in their localities.

- In addition to providing certain facilities, the government also operates through laws to ensure that concrete steps are taken to end inequity in the system. One such law/policy is the reservation policy that today is both significant and highly contentious. The laws which reserve seats in education and government employment for Dalits and Adivasis are based on an important argument- that in a society like ours, where for centuries sections of the population have been denied opportunities to learn and to work in order to develop new skills or vocations, a democratic government needs to step in and assist these sections.

THE SCHEDULED CASTES AND THE SCHEDULED TRIBES (PREVENTION OF ATROCITIES) ACT, 1989

- This Act was framed in 1989 in response to demands made by Dalits and others that the government must take seriously the ill treatment and humiliation Dalits and tribal groups face in an everyday sense. While such treatment had persisted for a long time, it had acquired a violent character in the late 1970s and 1980s

6   Our Constitution

WHAT IS CONSTITUTION?

- The constitution is a political frame based on which principles or laws of a country are formulated. Under the constitution, the rights and duties of citizens are described. The relationship of people with governments is decided by the constitution. It comprises a number of articles about the state, specifying how the state is to be constituted and what norms it should follow.

TYPES OF CONSTITUTION

Written and Unwritten

- United Kingdom - do not have one single document that can be called the Constitution. Rather they have a series of documents and decisions that, taken collectively, are referred to as the constitution. Unlike most modern states, Britain does not have a codified constitution but an unwritten one formed of Acts of Parliament, court judgments and conventions.

FUNCTIONS OF A CONSTITUTION

1. Constitution allows coordination and assurance

- The first function of a constitution is to provide a set of basic rules that allow for minimal coordination amongst members of a society

- In the absence of some basic rules ,every individual would be insecure simply because they would not know what members of this group could do to each other. Who could claim rights over what. Any group will need some basic rules that are publicly promulgated and known to all members of that group to achieve a minimal degree of coordination. If citizens have no assurance that others will follow these rules, they will themselves have no reason to follow these rules. legally enforceable gives an assurance to everybody that others will follow these, for if they do not do so, they will be punished. Group can live together if they can agree on some basic rules

2. Specification of decision making powers

- The second function of a constitution is to specify who has the power to make decisions in a society. It decides how the government will be constituted.
- Constitution is a body of fundamental principles according to which a state is constituted or governed. The constitution specifies the basic allocation of power in a society. It decides who gets to decide what the laws will be.
- In monarchical constitution, a monarch decides .In old Soviet Union constitution - one single party was given the power to decide but in Democratic constitutions ,the people get to decide.

3. Limitations on the powers of government

- The third function of a constitution is to set some limits on what a government can impose on its citizens. These limits are fundamental in the sense that government may never trespass them.

4. Aspirations and goals of a society

- The fourth function of a constitution is to enable the government to fulfil the aspirations of a society and create conditions for a just society.
- Government can't violates Fundamental rights. Exact content and interpretation of these rights varies from constitution to constitution. But most constitutions will protect a basic cluster of rights. Citizens will be protected from being arrested arbitrarily and for no reason. This is one basic limitation upon the power of government. Citizens will normally have the right to some basic liberties: to freedom of speech, freedom of conscience, freedom of association, freedom to conduct a trade or business etc. In practice, these rights can be limited during times of national emergency and the constitution specifies the circumstances under which these rights may be withdrawn. Indian Constitution provides an enabling framework for the government to do certain positive things to express the aspirations and goals of society.
- Indian Constitution ensures each individual to lead a life of minimal dignity, social self-respect, minimum material well-being, education etc. Indian Constitution enables the government to take positive welfare measures some of which are legally enforceable.
- Fundamental Rights/ The Directive Principles of State of Policy fulfil certain aspirations of the people.

CONSTITUTION EXPRESSES FUNDAMENTAL IDENTITY OF A PEOPLE

- It provides basic set of norms on how one should be governed/ who should be governed and forms a collective identity

1. Political identity

- There were many sets of identities prior to a constitution.
- By agreeing to certain basic norms and principles one constitutes one's basic political identity

2. Moral identity

- The constitution sets authoritative constraints upon what one may or may not do.
- It defines the fundamental values that we may not trespass.
- So the constitution also gives one a moral identity/ common set of Right and Wrong.

3. National Identity

- Nations weave together the diverse groups that reside within the nation in different ways.
- Indian Constitution does not make ethnic identity a criterion for citizenship /legacy of accommodation

Making a constitution effective depends upon many factors like

- Mode of promulgation - People who enacted the constitution credible?
- The substantive provisions of a constitution - Does the constitution give everyone some reason to go along with ?
- Balanced institutional design - Power was intelligently organised?
- Constitution must strike the right balance between flexibility and Rigidity - Is the constitution the locus of people's hopes and aspiration?

HOW WAS THE INDIAN CONSTITUTION MADE?

- By the Constituent Assembly which had been elected for undivided India.
- First sitting of the Constituent assembly - 9 December1946
- Its members were chosen by indirect election by the members of the Provincial Legislative Assemblies
- Constituent Assembly was established under the Government of India Act, 1935.
- The Constituent Assembly was composed in accordance with Cabinet Mission.

Cabinet Mission Plan

- Province/Princely State/group of States were allotted seats proportional to their respective population
- Ratio of 1:10,00,000.
- Provinces (under direct British rule) - to elect 292 members
- Princely States were allotted a minimum of 93 seats.
- Distribution of seats in each province - Muslims, Sikhs and general (in proportion to their respective populations.)
- Members of each community in the Provincial Legislative Assembly elected their own representatives by the method of proportional representation with single transferable vote.
- The method of selection in the case of representatives of Princely States was to be determined by consultation.

Composition of the Constituent Assembly

- After Partition (3 June 1947 Mountbatten plan)
- Pakistan ceased to be member of the Constituent Assembly.
- The number of members in the Assembly was reduced to 299.
- Constitution was adopted on 26 November 1949.
- On 24 January 1950 signature to the Constitution finally passed.
- The Constitution came into force on 26 January 1950

Constituent Assembly – Working procedure

- Constituent Assembly eight major Committees on different subjects.
- Usually, Jawaharlal Nehru, Rajendra Prasad, Sardar Patel or B.R. Ambedkar chaired these Committees.
- These were not men who agreed with each other on many things.
- Ambedkar had been a bitter critic of the Congress and Gandhi, accusing them of not doing enough for the upliftment of Scheduled Castes.
- Patel and Nehru disagreed on many issues.
- Nevertheless, they all worked together.
- Committee - drafted provisions of the Constitution which were then subjected to debate by the entire Assembly.
- The Assembly met for one hundred and sixty
- six days, spread over two years and eleven months.
- Its sessions were open to the press and the public alike.

Constituent assembly consensus

- Background consensus on the main principles the Constitution should enshrine.
- These principles were forged during the long struggle for freedom.
- The Constituent Assembly was giving concrete shape and form to the principles it had inherited from the nationalist movement
- The nationalist movement brought to the Constituent Assembly is the Objectives Resolution (the resolution that defined the aims of the Assembly) moved by Nehru in 1946.
- This resolution encapsulated the aspirations and values behind the Constitution.
- Based on this resolution, our Constitution gave institutional expression to these fundamental commitments: equality, liberty, democracy, sovereignty and a cosmopolitan identity.

Objectives Resolution

- Introduced by Nehru
- Outlined the Assembly's goals in 1946 before the constitution-making process began.

- The aims and principles that drove the creation of the Constitution were embodied in this resolution.
- Provided the foundation for India's Constitution.
- Institutionalized the essential values of equality, liberty, democracy and sovereignty
- Carry out the many promises made by the nationalist movement to the Indian people.
- The Preamble to the Constitution is based on this resolution, accepted on January 22, 1947.
- The essential framework of our constitution is included in the preamble's goals.
- It emphasizes the Indian constitution's key ideas and philosophy.
- It is regarded as the constitution's soul.

Borrowing from other constitutional traditions

- Makers of our constitutions - learn from experiments and experiences of other countries
- they borrowed a number of provisions from different countries.
- Each provision of the Constitution had to be defended on grounds that it was suited to Indian problems and aspirations.
- India was extremely lucky to have an Assembly that instead of being parochial in its outlook could take the best available everywhere in the world and make it their own.

Our constitution has features taken from the Government of India Act, 1935.

Those features are:

- Federal Scheme
- Office of governor
- Judiciary
- Public Service Commissions
- Emergency provisions
- Administrative details

7 Fundamental Rights, Duties and Directive Principles of State Policy

CONCEPT

- It is basic human rights guaranteed to all citizens.
- It is applied without discrimination on the basis of race, religion, gender, etc.

WHY ARE THEY CALLED FUNDAMENTAL RIGHTS?

These rights are called fundamental rights because of two reasons:

1. They are enshrined in the Constitution which guarantees them
2. They are justiciable (enforceable by courts). In case of a violation, a person can approach a court of law.

FUNDAMENTAL RIGHTS(FR) – FEATURES

- Article 12 to 35 contained in Part III of the Constitution
- It secures Political Freedom
- It helps in all round development.
- Without Fundamental Rights we can't survive in dignified manner
- Fundamental Rights check on Ultimate power of state.
- Fundamental Rights are not absolute rights. Reasonable restrictions can be imposed.
- Article 20/21 – can't suspended in emergency.
- Article 19 – can be suspended during emergency.
- It is Protected and guaranteed by the Constitution of the country – ARTICLE 32
- Can only be changed by amending the Constitution itself.
- Part of the basic structure of the Constitution
- It cannot be waived-off by an individual.
- If these are violated then an individual can move to Supreme Court or High Court
- The remedy to move to SC in case of violation of FR is itself a fundamental right.(32)
- Individual has these rights against the state
- Judiciary has the powers and responsibility to protect the fundamental rights from violations by actions of the government.

- Executive as well as legislative actions can be declared illegal by the judiciary if these violate the fundamental rights
- Fundamental rights are not absolute or unlimited rights.
- Government can put reasonable restrictions on the exercise of our fundamental rights.

CONSTITUTIONAL/ORDINARY LEGAL RIGHTS

- Legal rights are protected and enforced by ordinary law of the country.
- May be changed by the legislature by ordinary
- process of law making.
- It is not a part of the Basic structure doctrine.
- It can be waived-off by an individual.
- If these are violated then an individual have to move to ordinary court first.
- These rights impose a corresponding obligation on the individual (and in some cases state too). For eg: Right to vote is a legal right

BILL OF RIGHTS

- Rights of the citizens mentioned in the constitution itself.
- It is Practiced in most democratic countries
- Such a list of rights called the 'bill of rights'.
- It prohibits government from acting against the rights of the individuals
- It ensures a remedy in case there is violation of these rights.
- Constitution protect the rights of the individual from person or private organisation.

FUNDAMENTAL RIGHTS IN DETAIL

Article 12

- Define State
- Executive and legislative – Union
- Executive and legislative – State
- Local authority
- Other authority – AAI/LIC/ONGC/PSUs

Article 13

- Constitution is Supreme
- Provision of Judicial Review

SIX FUNDAMENTAL RIGHTS

1. **Right to Equality (Art 14-18)**
   - Equality before law
   - equal protection of laws (Art 14)
   - Prohibition of discrimination on grounds of religion, race, caste, sex or place of birth (Art 15)
   - equal access to shops, hotels, wells, tanks, bathing ghats, roads etc.

- Equality of opportunity in public employment (Art 16)
- Abolition of Untouchability (Art 17)
- Abolition of titles (Art 18)

2. Right to Freedom (Art 19-22)

- Protection of Right to (Art 19)
- freedom of speech and expression; Art 19(1) (A)
- assemble peacefully; Art 19(1) (B)
- form associations/unions; Art 19(1) (C)
- move freely throughout the territory of India; Art 19(1) (D)
- reside and settle in any part of India; Art 19(1) (E)
- practise any profession, or to carry on any occupation, trade or business. Art 19(1) (G)
- Protection in respect of conviction for offences (Art 20)
- Right to life and personal liberty (Art 21)
- Right to education (Art 21-A)
- Protection against arrest and detention in certain cases (Art 22)

3. Right against Exploitation (Article 23 -24)

- Prohibition of traffic in human beings and forced labour (Art 23)
- Prohibition of employment of children in hazardous jobs (Art 24)

4. Right to Freedom of Religion (Article 25 – 28)

- Freedom of conscience and free profession, practice and propagation of religion (Art 25)
- Freedom to manage religious affairs (Art 26)
- Freedom to pay taxes for promotion of any particular religion (Art 27)
- Freedom to attend religious instruction or worship in certain educational institutions (Art 28)

5. Cultural and Educational Rights (Article 29 – 30)

- Protection of language, culture of minorities (Art 29)
- Right of minorities to establish educational institutions (Art 30)

6. Right to Constitutional Remedies

- Right to move the courts to issue directions/orders/writs for enforcement of rights (Art 32)

The courts can issue various special orders known as writs

1. *Habeas corpus: to bring the body*
   - court orders that the arrested person should be presented before it.
   - It can also order to set free an arrested person if the manner or grounds of arrest are not lawful or satisfactory.

2. *Mandamus : to give mandate/do your job*
   - This writ is issued when the court finds that a particular office holder is not doing legal duty and thereby is infringing on the right of an individual.

3. *Quo Warranto : By What authority or warrant.*
   - If the court finds that a person is holding office but is not entitled to hold that office, it issues the writ of quo warranto and restricts that person from acting as an office holder.

4. *Prohibition : to forbid*
   - This writ is issued by a higher court (High Court or Supreme Court) when a lower court has considered a case going beyond its jurisdiction.

5. *Certiorari : produce the certificate*
   - Under this writ, the court orders a lower court or another authority to transfer a matter pending before it to the higher authority or court.

The Verdict given in Kesavananda Bharati Case 1973

- Given the basic structure of the Constitution doctrine
- Court said that nobody, not even the Parliament (through amendment)—can violate the basic structure.
- Court also said that the right to property was not part of basic structure
- Court reserved to itself the right to decide whether various matters are part of the basic structure of the Constitution.

The 'basic structure' doctrine has since been interpreted to include

- the supremacy of the Constitution,
- the rule of law,
- Independence of the judiciary,
- doctrine of separation of powers,
- sovereign democratic republic,
- the parliamentary system of government,
- the principle of free and fair elections,
- welfare state, etc.

DIRECTIVE PRINCIPLES OF STATE POLICY (ARTICLE 36-51)

- Some guidelines were incorporated in the Constitution but they were not made legally enforceable
- these guidelines are 'non-justiciable' i.e., parts of the Constitution that cannot be enforced by the judiciary.
- moral force behind these guidelines would ensure that the government would take them seriously.
- people would also hold the governments responsible for implementing these directives.

Directive Principles lists mainly three things:

- the goals and objectives that we as a society should adopt;
- certain rights that individuals should enjoy apart from the Fundamental Rights; and
- certain policies that the government should adopt.

Governments actions to give effect to some Directive Principles of State Policy.

- Zamindari abolition bills
- Nationalised banks
- Enacted numerous factory laws
- Fixed minimum wages
- Cottage and small industries were promoted
- Provisions for reservation for the uplift of SC/ST
- Right to education
- Formation PRI
- Mid-day meal scheme etc.

FUNDAMENTAL DUTIES OF CITIZENS

- In 1976, the 42nd amendment to the Constitution
- Fundamental Duties of Citizens inserted
- In all, ten duties were enumerated.
- Constitution does not say anything about enforcing these duties.
- As citizens, we must abide by the Constitution, defend our country, promote harmony among all citizens, protect the environment.

RELATIONSHIP BETWEEN FUNDAMENTAL RIGHTS AND DIRECTIVE PRINCIPLES

- Complementary to each other.
- Fundamental Rights restrain the government from doing certain things
- Directive Principles exhort the government to do certain things.
- Fundamental Rights -protect the rights of individuals
- Directive principles ensure the well-being of the entire society.

8 Elections and Democracy

ELECTIONS AND DEMOCRACY

- Election - Method followed to choose the representatives
- Democracy - Of the People, By the People, For the People

DEMOCRACY – DIRECT AND INDIRECT

- Direct - Citizens directly participate in day-to-day decision making and in running government (gram sabha)
- Indirect - Rule by the people means rule by people's representatives – Proportional Representation/First Past the Post (FPTP)

The constitution of a democratic country lays down some basic rules about elections.

- Who is eligible to vote?
- Who is eligible to contest?
- Who is to supervise elections?
- How do the voters choose their representatives?
- How are the votes to be counted and representatives elected?

ELECTION SYSTEM IN INDIA

1. First Past the Post System

Under this system:

- Entire country is divided into 543 constituencies
- Each constituency elects one representative
- Candidate who secures the highest number of votes in that constituency is declared elected. Candidate need not secure a majority of the votes. This method is called the First Past the Post (FPTP)system/Plurality System.

- Indian Constitution follows Federal System in which there are two types of government – Centre and State
- Centre Govt comprises of – Lok Sabha + Rajya Sabha

Types of Elections in India

- 1. General Election/ Lok Sabha Election – 543 seats, directly elected by public
- 2. Rajya Sabha Election – indirectly elected by public
- 3. State Legislative Election – MLAs of state

2. Proportional Representation (PR)

Considering the example of Israel to understand PR

- Israel Parliament – Knesset
- Election - Every four years.
- Voters vote for the party and not for the candidates.
- In Israel once the votes are counted, each party is allotted the share of seats in the parliament in proportion to its share of votes
- Each party fills its quota of seats by picking those many of its nominees from a preference list that has been declared before the elections.
- This system of elections is called the Proportional Representation (PR) system.
- In this system a party gets the same proportion of seats as its proportion of votes.
- Smaller parties - get representation in the legislature.
- Leads to a multi-party coalition government.

Proportional Representation – Two variations

First

- Entire country - one constituency and seats are allocated to each party according to its share of votes in the national election. /eg Israel or Netherlands

Second

- Country is divided into several multi-member
- E.g. - constituencies as in Argentina and Portugal.
- Each party prepares a list of candidates for each constituency,

Proportional Representation – Features

- In both these variations, voters exercise their preference for a party and not a candidate.
- Seats in a constituency - distributed on the basis of votes polled by a party
- Representatives from a constituency - different parties.

Proportional Representation (Indian Version)

- Adopted PR system on a limited scale for indirect elections.
- The Constitution prescribes a third and complex variation of the PR system
- It is for the election of President, Vice President, and for the election to the Rajya Sabha and Vidhan Parishads.

How does PR work in Rajya Sabha elections

- PR (third variant) - Single Transferable Vote system (STV)
- Followed for Rajya Sabha elections.
- Every State - specific quota of seats in the Rajya Sabha.
- Members elected - by the respective State legislative assemblies.
- The voters are the MLAs in that State.
- Every voter is required to rank candidates according to her or his preference.
- To be declared the winner, a candidate must secure a minimum quota of votes, which is determined by a formula

State Specific quota of seats in the Rajya Sabha

State/UT Name	No. Seats	State/UT Name	No. Seats
Andhra Pradesh	11	Meghalaya	1
Arunachal Pradesh	1	Mizoram	1
Assam	7	Nagaland	1
Bihar	16	NCT to Delhi	3
Chhattisgarh	5	Odisha	10
Goa	1	Puducherry	1
Gujarat	11	Punjab	7
Haryana	5	Rajasthan	10
Himachal Pradesh	3	Sikkim	1
Jammu and Kashmir	4	Tamil Nadu	18
Jharkhand	6	Telangana	7
Karnataka	12	Tripura	1
Kerala	9	Uttar Pradesh	31
Madhya Pradesh	11	Uttarakhand	3
Maharashtra	19	Westest Bengal	16
Manipur	1	Presidential nominees	12
	122		123
Total Number of Seats = 122 + 123 = 245			

Why did India adopt the FPTP system?

- Proportional Representation is a complicated system(PR) / FPTP system - simplicity
- It may work in a small country, but difficult to implement in a big country like India.
- The FPTP system offers voters a choice not simply between parties but specific candidates.
- In PR systems, voters to choose a party and the representatives are elected on the basis of party lists.
- No one representative who represents and is responsible for one locality.
- In FPTP, the voters know who their own representative is and can hold him or her accountable.
- PR based election may not be suitable for giving a stable government in a parliamentary system.
- PR system - No clear majority because seats in the legislature would be divided on the basis of share of votes.

RAJYA SABHA – PR(STV)

- Also known as – Permanent House/Upper House /Council Of States
- The Rajya Sabha should consist of not more than 250 members - 238 members representing the States and Union Territories, and 12 members nominated by the President. Rajya Sabha is a permanent body and is not subject to dissolution.
- At present there are 245 Members in which – 238 are elected and 12 are nominated by the president (Art./Science/Literature/Social Service)
- 1/3 member retire every 2 years.
- Term - 6 years

LOK SABHA - FPTP

- Temporary House as it dissolves after 5 years.
- Every 5 years – new election through FPTP
- Maximum strength of the House is 552 members - 530 members to represent the States, 20 members to represent the Union Territories, and 2 members to be nominated by the President from the Anglo-Indian Community.
- At present, the strength of the House is 543
- 545 Seats – 543 elected and 2 Anglo- Indians nominated
- For making government – 272 seats are required.

FPTP system – Benefits

- Parliamentary government to function smoothly and effectively /stable government.
- Gives the largest party or coalition some extra bonus seats /voting share
- Encourages voters from different social groups to come together to win an election in a locality.
- PR system would encourage each community to form its own nation-wide party
- It has helped larger parties to win clear majorities at the centre and the State level
- FPTP in India is slightly different. – one party dominance/existed small parties/1989 multi-party coalitions – beneficial for smaller party

- Discouraged political parties that get all their votes only from one caste or community.
- FPTP system results in a two-party system.
- Difficult for new parties or the third party to enter the competition and share power

RESERVATION OF CONSTITUENCIES

- In this system, all voters in a constituency are eligible to vote but the candidates must belong to only a particular community or social section for which the seat is reserved.
- The Constitution provides for reservation of seats in the Lok Sabha and State Legislative Assemblies for the Scheduled Castes and Scheduled Tribes.
- This provision was made initially for a period of 10 years and as a result of successive constitutional amendments, has been extended up to 2020.
- The Parliament can take a decision to further extend it, when the period of reservation expires.
- Of the 543 elected seats in the Lok Sabha, 84 are reserved for Scheduled Castes and 47 are reserved for Scheduled Tribes (as on 26 January 2019)

Who decides which constituency is to be reserved? - Delimitation Commission

- Appointed by the President of India and works in collaboration with the Election Commission of India.
- It is appointed for the purpose of drawing up the boundaries of constituencies all over the country.
- A quota of constituencies to be reserved in each State is fixed depending on the proportion of SC or ST in that State.

Delimitation Commission

- The Delimitation Commission is a high-level body set up by an act of the Parliament.
- The Delimitation Commission Act was enacted in 1952.
- It is appointed by the country's President.
- It works in tandem with the Election Commission of India.
- The main task of the commission is redrawing the boundaries of the various assembly and Lok Sabha constituencies based on a recent census.
- Following the 84th amendment to the Constitution, in 2002, Delimitation is to be done after 2026 if not postponed.
- The base year will be 2021 population.
- The most recent delimitation commission was set up on 12 July 2002 after the 2001 census
- The present delimitation of parliamentary constituencies within states, has been done on the basis of the 2001 census, under the provisions of Delimitation Act, 2002.
- The Constitution of India was specifically amended (84th amendment) in 2002, not to have interstate delimitation of constituencies till 2026.
- Thus, the present constituencies carved out on the basis of the 2001 census shall continue to be in operation till 2026 and later it can be done on the basis of population 2021.

- The total number of seats in the Parliament and the Legislative Assemblies fixed as per the census of 1971 was not changed.
- Constitution of India has put a cap on the maximum number of seats in the Lok Sabha to 550 and Rajya Sabha to 250.

RIGHT TO VOTE AND RIGHT TO CONTEST

Right to Vote

- All adult citizens of the country must be eligible to vote in the elections.
- This is known as universal adult franchise.
- Adult – 21 years (Till 1989)/ An amendment to the Constitution in 1989, reduced the eligibility age to 18.
- Our Constitution makers had a firm belief in the ability and worth of all adult citizens.

Right to Contest

- All citizens have the right to stand for election and become the representative of the people.
- Age - Lok Sabha or Assembly election, a candidate must be at least 25 years old.
- No restrictions of income, education or class or gender on the right to contest elections.
- Our system of election is open to all citizen

ELECTION COMMISSION OF INDIA

- To assist the Election Commission of India there is a Chief Electoral Officer in every state.
- The Election Commission is not responsible for the conduct of local body elections.
- The Election Commission of India can either be a single member or a multi-member body.
- Till 1989 -single member./before 1989 general elections, two Election Commissioners were appointed, making the body multi-member/ after the elections again single member status.
- In 1993, two Election Commissioners were once again appointed and the Commission became multi-member
- Chief Election Commissioner (CEC) presides over the Election Commission, but does not have more powers than the other Election Commissioners.
- The CEC and the two Election Commissioners have equal powers to take all decisions relating to elections as a collective body.
- They are appointed by the President of India on the advice of the Council of Ministers.
- The Constitution ensures the security of the tenure of the CEC and Election Commissioners.
- They are appointed for a six year term or continue till the age of 65, whichever is earlier
- They are appointed for a six year term or continue till the age of 65, whichever is earlier.
- The CEC can be removed before the expiry of the term, by the President if both Houses of Parliament make such a recommendation with a special majority.
- This is done to ensure that a ruling party cannot remove a CEC who refuses to favour it in elections.
- The Election Commissioners can be removed by the President of India.

Election Commission of India - Functions

- Supervises the preparation of up-to-date voters' list.
- determines the timing of elections and prepares the election schedule.
- Implement a model code of conduct for parties and candidates.
- It can order a re-poll in a specific constituency.
- It can also order a recount of votes
- The Election Commission accords recognition to political parties and allots symbols to each of them.

ELECTORAL REFORMS

- Our system of elections should be changed from the FPTP to some variant of the PR system.
- There should be a special provision to ensure that at least one- third women are elected to the parliament and assemblies.
- stricter provisions to control the role of money in electoral politics.
- The elections expenses should be paid by the government out of a special fund.
- Candidates with any criminal case should be barred from contesting elections, even if their appeal is pending before a court.
- There should be complete ban on the use of caste and religious appeals in the campaign.
- There should be a law to regulate the functioning of political parties and to ensure that they function in a transparent and democratic manner.

9 Executive

ORGANS OF THE GOVERNMENT

Executive/Legislative/Judiciary

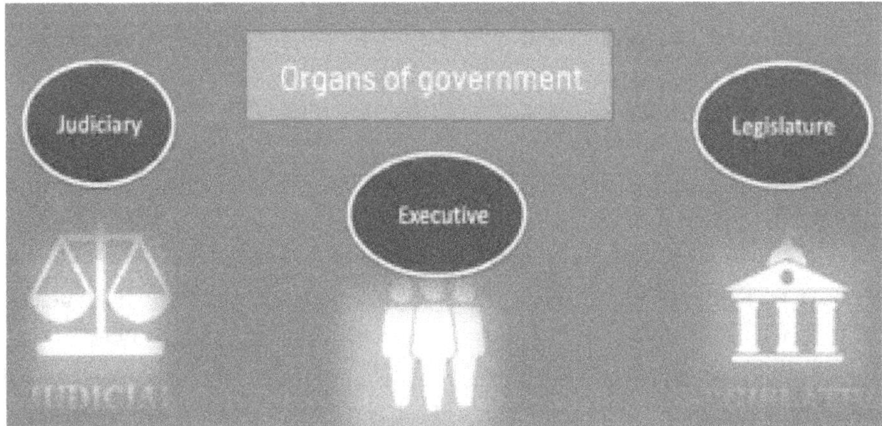

- Perform the functions of the government
- Maintain law and order
- Welfare of the people.
- Work in coordination with each other and maintain a balance among themselves.
- In a parliamentary system, executive and the legislature are interdependent: the legislature controls the executive, and, in turn, is controlled by the executive

What is an Executive

- The Union executive consists of the President, the Vice-President, and the Council of Ministers with the Prime Minister as the head to aid and advise the President.
- Responsible for the implementation of laws and policies adopted by the legislature.
- Involved in framing of policy.

- Executives consist of - presidents, prime ministers, cabinet and other ministers , administrative machinery (civil servants).
- Political executive - overall responsibility of government policy/Head of govt.
- Permanent executive - day to day administration
- Executive – Real Executive(Head of State) and Ceremonial Executive (Head of government)

Types of Executive

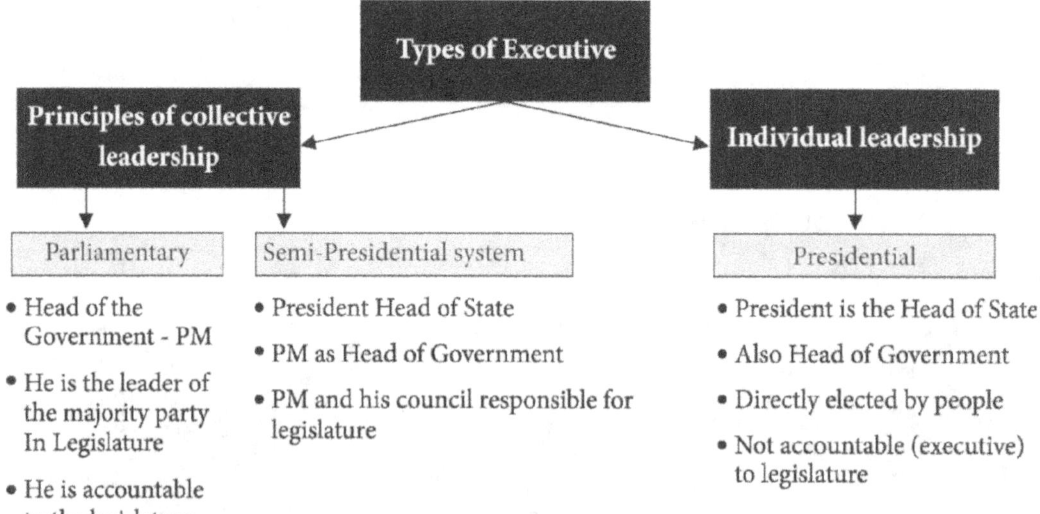

- USA has a presidential system and executive powers are in the hands of the president.
- Canada has a parliamentary democracy with a constitutional monarchy where Queen Elizabeth II is the formal chief of state and the prime minister is the head of government.
- In France, both the president and the prime minister are a part of the semi- presidential system. The president appoints the prime minister as well as the ministers but cannot dismiss them as they are responsible to the parliament.
- Japan has a parliamentary system with the Emperor as the head of the state and the prime minister as the head of government.
- Italy has a parliamentary system with the president as the formal head of state and the prime minister as the head of government.
- Russia has a semi-presidential system where president is the head of state and prime minister, who is appointed by the president, is the head of government.
- Germany has a parliamentary system in which president is the ceremonial head of state and the chancellor is the head of government.
- In a presidential system, the president is the Head of state as well as head of government.
- In this system the office of president is very powerful, both in theory and practice (eg. United States, Brazil)

Presidential System

- Under the system of Executive Presidency, people directly elect the President.
- President and the Prime Minister belong to the same political party or to different political parties.
- The President has vast powers under the constitution.
- The President chooses the Prime Minister from the party that has a majority in the Parliament.
- President has the power to remove the Prime Minister, or ministers.
- President - Head of State and the Commander-in- Chief of the Armed Forces, / Head of the Government.
- Elected for a term of six years, the President cannot be removed except by a resolution in the parliament passed by at least two-thirds of the total number of Members of Parliament.

Parliamentary System

- Prime minister is the head of government.
- President or a monarch who is the nominal Head of state.
- Role of president or monarch is primarily ceremonial and prime minister along with the cabinet wields effective power.
- Countries with such system include Germany, Italy, Japan, United Kingdom as well as Portugal.

Semi – Presidential System

- It has both a president and a prime minister but unlike the parliamentary system the president may possess significant day-to-day powers.
- President and the prime minister may belong to the same party and at times they may belong to two different parties and thus, would be opposed to each other.
- Countries with such a system include France, Russia, Sri Lanka, etc.

PARLIAMENTARY EXECUTIVE IN INDIA

- Parliamentary form - many mechanisms that ensure that the executive will be answerable to and controlled by the legislature or people's representatives.
- Constitution adopted the parliamentary system of executive for the governments both at the national and State levels.
- President who is the formal Head of the state of India and the Prime Minister and the Council of Ministers, run the government at the national level.
- At the State level, the executive comprises the Governor and the Chief Minister and Council of Ministers.
- The Constitution of India vests the executive power of the Union formally in the President.
- In reality, the President exercises these powers through the Council of Ministers headed by the Prime Minister
- The President is elected for a period of five years.

- But there is no direct election by the people for the office of President.
- The President is elected indirectly.
- This means that the president is elected not by the ordinary citizens but by the elected MLAs and MPs.
- This election takes place in accordance with the principle of proportional representation with single transferable vote.
- The President can be removed from office only by Parliament by following the procedure for impeachment.
- This procedure requires a special majority
- The only ground for impeachment is violation of the Constitution.

Power and Position of President

- President - formal head of the government.
- President has wide ranging executive, legislative, judicial and emergency powers.
- In a parliamentary system, these powers are in reality used by the President only on the advice of the Council of Ministers.
- The Prime Minister and the Council of Ministers have support of the majority in the Lok Sabha and they are the real executive.

Discretionary Powers of the President

- The President has a right to be informed of all important matters and deliberations of the Council of Ministers.
- The Prime Minister is obliged to furnish all the information that the President may call for.

President can exercise the powers using his or her own discretion.

First

- President can send back the advice given by the Council of Ministers and ask the Council to reconsider the decision.
- In doing this, the President acts on his (or her) own discretion

Secondly

- The President also has veto power by which he can withhold or refuse to give assent to Bills (other than Money Bill) passed by the Parliament.
- The President can send the bill back to the Parliament asking it to reconsider the bill.
- This 'veto' power is limited because, if the Parliament passes the same bill again and sends it back to the President, then, the President has to give assent to that bill.
- No mention in the Constitution about the time limit within which the President must send the bill back for reconsideration.
- President can just keep the bill pending with him without any time limit.

- This gives the President an informal power to use the veto in a very effective manner. This is sometimes referred to as 'pocket veto'.
- Zail Singh, the President of India from 1982 until 1987, exercised a pocket veto to prevent the Indian Post Office (Amendment) Bill from becoming law.

Third

- Presidential intervention to constitute governments
- When no party has a clear majority, the President has the additional responsibility of making a choice and appointing the Prime Minister to run the government of the country.
- In such a situation, the President has to use his own discretion in judging who really may have the support of the majority or who can actually form and run the government.
- 1989 to 1998, no single party or coalition attained a majority in the Lok Sabha

The Vice President of India

- The Vice President is elected for five years.
- His election method is similar to that of the President, the only difference is that members of State legislatures are not part of the electoral college.
- The Vice President may be removed from his office by a resolution of the Rajya Sabha passed by a majority and agreed to by the Lok Sabha.
- The Vice President acts as the ex- officio Chairman of the Rajya Sabha and takes over the office of the President when there is a vacancy by reasons of death, resignation, removal by impeachment or otherwise.
- The Vice President acts as the President only until a new President is elected.
- B. D. Jatti acted as President on the death of Fakhruddin Ali Ahmed until a new President was elected.

WHY DO WE NEED A PRESIDENT?

- In a parliamentary system, the Council of Ministers is dependent on the support of the majority in the legislature.
- Council of Ministers may be removed at any time and a new Council of Ministers will have to be put in place.
- Such a situation requires a Head of the state who has a fixed term, who may be empowered to appoint the Prime Minister and who may symbolically represent the entire country.
- This is exactly the role of the President in ordinary circumstances.
- Besides, when no party has a clear majority, the President has the additional responsibility of making a choice and appointing the Prime Minister to run the government of the country.

COUNCIL OF MINISTERS

- President exercises his powers only on the advice of the Council of Ministers.
- The Council of Ministers is headed by the Prime Minister.

- As head of the Council of Ministers, the Prime Minister becomes the most important functionary of the government in our country.
- In the parliamentary form of executive, it is essential that the Prime Minister has the support of the majority in the Lok Sabha.
- This support by the majority also makes the Prime Minister very powerful.
- The moment this support of the majority is lost, the Prime Minister loses the office.
- A leader who has the support of the majority is appointed by the President as Prime Minister.
- The Prime Minister then decides who will be the ministers in the Council of Ministers.
- The Prime Minister allocates ranks and portfolios to the ministers.
- Depending upon the seniority and political importance, the ministers are given the ranks of cabinet minister, minister of State or deputy minister.
- The Prime Minister and all the ministers have to be members of the Parliament.
- If someone becomes a minister or Prime Minister without being an MP, such a person has to get elected to the Parliament within six months.
- The Council of Ministers is collectively responsible to the Lok Sabha.
- This provision means that a Ministry which loses confidence of the Lok Sabha is obliged to resign.
- Collective responsibility is based on the principle of the solidarity of the cabinet.
- If a minister does not agree with a policy or decision of the cabinet, he or she must either accept the decision or resign.
- It is binding on all ministers to pursue or agree to a policy for which there is collective responsibility.
- The Council comes into existence only after the Prime Minister has taken the oath of office.
- The death or resignation of the Prime Minister automatically brings about the dissolution of the Council of Ministers but the demise, dismissal or resignation of a minister only creates a ministerial vacancy
- The Prime Minister acts as a link between the Council of Ministers on the one hand and the President as well as the Parliament on the other.

PERMANENT EXECUTIVE: BUREAUCRACY

Executive organ of the government

- Prime Minister, the ministers and a large organisation called the bureaucracy or the administrative machinery.
- Permanent executive - Trained and skilled officers who work as permanent employees of the government are assigned the task of assisting the ministers in formulating policies and implementing these policies.
- The bureaucracy is an instrument through which welfare policies of the government must reach the people

Indian Bureaucracy

- India has established professional administrative machinery.
- The bureaucracy is expected to be politically neutral.
- This means that the bureaucracy will not take any political position on policy matters.
- Indian bureaucracy consists of the All-India services, State services, employees of the local governments, and technical and managerial staff running public sector undertakings.
- They impartially selected on the basis of merit.
- Union Public Service Commission has been entrusted with the task of conducting the process of recruitment of the civil servants for the government of India.
- Similar public service commissions are provided for the States also.
- An IAS or IPS officer is assigned to a particular State -works under the supervision of the State government.
- IAS or IPS officers are appointed by the central government
- Only the central government can take disciplinary action against them.
- Key administrative officers of the States are under the supervision and control of the central government.
- Apart from the IAS and the IPS officers appointed by the UPSC, the administration of the State is looked after by officers appointed through the State Public Service Commissions.
- The bureaucracy is an instrument through which welfare policies of the government must reach the people.
- Members of the Public Service Commissions are appointed for a fixed term.
- Their removal or suspension is subject to a thorough enquiry made by a judge of the Supreme Court.
- Constitution has provided for reservation of jobs for the Dalits , Adivasis, women and other backward classes.
- These provisions ensure that the bureaucracy would be more representative
- Persons selected by the UPSC for Indian Administrative Service and Indian Police Service constitute the backbone of the higher level bureaucracy in the States.

10 Legislature

LEGISLATURE

- It is a law making body.

- Centre of all democratic political process.

- Actions involved - walkouts, protests, demonstration, unanimity, concern and co-operation.

- Helps people in holding the representatives accountable.

National legislature - Bicameral legislature

- Council of States/Rajya Sabha

- House of the People/Lok Sabha

Unicameral or Bicameral legislature in States

- States have the option of establishing either a unicameral or bicameral legislature.(art168)

- At present only six States have a bicameral legislature.

- Andhra Pradesh, Bihar, Karnataka, Maharashtra, Telangana, and Uttar Pradesh

- Legislature comprises of – Governor +Vidhan Sabha + Vidhan Parishad (not mandatory)

WHY DO WE NEED TWO HOUSES OF PARLIAMENT?

- To give representation to all sections in the society

- To give representation to all geographical regions or parts of the country.

- A bicameral legislature makes it possible to have every decision reconsidered.

- Every decision taken by one house goes to the other house for its decision.

- Every bill and policy would be discussed twice.

- Double check on every matter.

- Even if one house takes a decision in haste, that decision will come for discussion in the other house and reconsideration will be possible.

Rajya Sabha

- Represents the States of India
- Indirectly elected body
- Twelve nominated members from the fields of literature, science, art and social service (art 80)
- Principles of representation – based on Population not on symmetrical representation.
- Term of six years/ re-elected.
- Every two years, one third members of the Rajya Sabha complete their term
- Rajya Sabha is never fully dissolved as it is a Permanent House of Parliament
- If Lok Sabha is dissolved then Rajya Sabha can be called for urgent business
- Rajya Sabha is also called as the Voice of elders, states/Spirit of Federalism

Lok Sabha

- Directly elected by the people
- Territorial constituencies - At present there are 543 constituencies
- One representative is elected from each constituency
- Universal adult suffrage where the value of vote of every individual would be equal to another.
- The Lok Sabha is elected for a period of five years.

WHAT DOES THE PARLIAMENT DO?

- Legislative Function - enacts legislations/Passing bills
- Control of Executive and ensuring its accountability –Question hour etc
- Financial Function – Passing of Money bill/Consolidated Fund of India grant of fund – Lok Sabha only ,Annual Financial Statement
- Representation - represents the divergent views of members
- Debating Function - highest forum of debate in the country
- Constituent Function –Constitutional amendments
- Electoral functions – elects President and Vice President of India
- Judicial functions - removal of President/VP/Judges of HC and SC

Special Powers of Rajya Sabha

- It signifies the representation to the States.
- It is also known as revisionary house
- One of its objectives is to protect the powers of the States.
- To remove or transfer any subject from the state list - approval of the Rajya Sabha is necessary (Article 249).
- To create additional All-India Services (Article 312).
- To endorse Emergency under Article 352 for a limited period when the Lok Sabha remains dissolved.

Powers exercised only by the Lok Sabha

- The Rajya Sabha cannot initiate, reject or amend money bills.
- The Council of Ministers is responsible to the Lok Sabha only
- Rajya Sabha can criticise the government but cannot remove it.
- Democratic form - the people are the final authority
- Removing a government and controlling the finances – role of people
- passing of non-money bills, constitutional amendments, and impeaching the President and removing the Vice President the powers of Lok Sabha and Rajya Sabha are co-equal

Difference between LS & RS

LOK SABHA	RAJYA SABHA
Makes Laws on matters included in Union List and Concurrent List. Can introduce and enact money and non money bills.	Considers and approves non money bills and suggests amendments to money bills.
Approves proposals for taxation, budgets and annual financial statements.	Approves constitutional amendments.
Controls the executive by asking questions, supplementary questions, resolutions and motions and through no confidence motion.	Exercises control over executive by asking questions, introducing motions and resolutions.
Amends the Constitution.	Participates in the election and removal of the President, Vice President, Judges of Supreme Court and High Court. It can alone initiate the procedure for removal of Vice President.
Approves the Proclamation of emergency.	Can give the Union parliament power to make laws on matters included in the State list.
Elects the President and Vice President and removes Judges of Supreme Court and High Court.	
Establishes committees and commissions and considers their reports.	

Law Making Process

- Cabinet approves the policy behind the legislation
- drafting the legislation begins.
- prepared by the concerned ministry.
- Introduced in the LS or RS/money bill only in Lok Sabha.
- Once passed there, it is sent to the Rajya Sabha.
- discussion on the bills takes place in the committees.
- The recommendation of the committee is then sent to the House
- Committees are referred to as miniature legislatures – 2nd stage
- In the third and final stage, the bill is voted upon.

- If a non-money bill is passed by one House, it is sent to the other House where it goes through exactly the same procedure.

- The Budget is classified as a 'money Bill,' by the Speaker of the Lok Sabha under Article 110 of the Constitution. The Rajya Sabha can recommend non-binding amendments to a money Bill, and it cannot be vetoed

- If there is disagreement between the two Houses on the proposed bill - Joint Session of Parliament.

- If it is a money bill, the Rajya Sabha can either approve the bill or suggest changes but cannot reject it.

- If it takes no action within 14 days the bill is deemed to have been passed.

- Amendments to the bill, suggested by Rajya Sabha, may or may not be accepted by the Lok Sabha

- When a bill is passed by both Houses, it is sent to the President for his assent.

- The assent of the President results in the enactment of a bill into a law

Joint Sitting of Indian parliament

- Article 108 of the Indian Constitution provides for a joint sitting of both Houses of Parliament. Accordingly, a joint session can be summoned when

If after a bill is passed by one House and transmitted to the other House –

1. The other House rejects this bill, or

2. The Houses do not agree on the amendments made to the bill, or

3. More than six months elapse with the bill being received by the other House without it being passed.

- Then, the President can summon a joint sitting unless the bill had elapsed because of the Lok Sabha's dissolution.

- Joint Sitting of Indian parliament has been called for only 3 bills: Dowry Prohibition Bill, 1961. Banking Service Commission (Repeal) Bill, 1978. Prevention of Terrorism Bill, 2002.

TYPES OF BILLS

- A bill is a draft of the proposed law. There can be different types of bills.

- When a non-minister proposes a bill, it is called private member's Bill

- A bill proposed by a minister is described as Government Bill.

There are three types of bills :

- Constitutional Amendment Bills

- Financial Bills

- Ordinary Bills

- Money Bills are Financial Bills which deal exclusively with the money matters mentioned in Article 110.

Money Bill

- Article 110 - money bill contains the imposition, abolition, remission, alteration or regulation of any tax.
- Contains tax proposals of the government
- New taxes and changes in rates of existing taxes.
- Government's expenditure, revenues, and borrowings.
- Imposition of local taxes doesn't come under the purview of the money bill.
- Payment of moneys into or the withdrawal of moneys from Consolidated Fund or the Contingency Fund of India
- Article 109 – Only in LS
- Consolidated fund of India contains direct and indirect taxes and loans taken by the government.
- Union government needs Parliamentary approval to deposit or take out money from it.
- This is done through the introduction of the money bill.
- Contingency fund of India is an emergency fund.
- Eg- to increase the salary of the President of the country -- which is drawn from the Consolidated Fund of India -- it will have to introduce a money bill.
- The Speaker of the Lok Sabha takes the final call if a bill is a money bill or not. And his decision cannot be challenged in any court of the country.

HOW DOES THE PARLIAMENT CONTROL THE EXECUTIVE?

1. Deliberation and discussion – Question hour/Zero hour
2. Approval or Refusal of laws
3. Financial control - LS can discuss the reasons for which the govt requires money can enquire into cases of misuse of funds on the basis of CAG and Auditor General and Public Accounts committees.
4. Legislature controls the policy of the government.
5. No confidence motion -ensure executive accountability
6. Parliament can effectively control the executive and ensure a more responsive government.

WHAT DO THE COMMITTEES OF PARLIAMENT DO?

- Parliamentary standing committees
- Role - law making, day-to-day business of the House
- appointment of committees for various legislative purposes
- in-depth study of the issue
- studying the demands for grants made by various ministries
- looking into expenditure incurred by various departments, investigating cases of corruption
- supervise the work of various departments, their budget, their expenditure

- Joint Parliamentary Committees (JPCs) - discussing a particular bill, investigating financial irregularities – Both LS/RS
- Parliamentary standing committees - over twenty such departmentally related committees.
- Standing Committees supervise the work of various departments, their budget, their expenditure and bills.

HOW DOES THE PARLIAMENT REGULATE ITSELF?

- The anti-defection law laid the process by which legislators may be disqualified on grounds of defection.
- An MLA or leader who switches party can avoid anti-defection law, only if one-third of the party legislators resign.
- Otherwise, any MLA or MP resigning from the party would stand disqualified and will lose membership.
- 52nd amendment act in 1985.
- anti-defection amendment.
- The presiding officer of the House is the authority who takes final decisions on all such cases.
- If it is proved that a member has 'defected', then such member loses the membership of the House.
- Defection - a member remains absent in the House when asked by the party leadership to remain present or votes against the instructions of the party or voluntarily leaves the membership of the party, it is deemed as defection.
- Anti-defection amendment has not been able to curb defections.

11

Judiciary

INDEPENDENCE OF JUDICIARY

What is meant by an independent judiciary?

- Disputes must be settled by an independent body in accordance with the principle of rule of law.
- Rule of law states that all individuals — rich and poor, men or women, forward or backward castes — are subjected to the same law.
- Judiciary is to protect rule of law and ensure supremacy of law.
- It safeguards rights of the individual, settles disputes in accordance with the law
- ensures that democracy does not give way to individual or group dictatorship.
- In order to be able to do all this, it is necessary that the judiciary is independent of any political pressures.

Independence of Judiciary

- Executive and legislature must not restrain the functioning of the judiciary
- other organs of the government should not interfere with the decision of the judiciary.
- judges must be able to perform their functions without fear or favour.
- Judiciary is a part of the democratic political structure of the country.
- It is therefore accountable to the Constitution

How can the independence of judiciary be provided and protected?

- Legislature is not involved in the process of appointment of judges.
- The judges have a fixed tenure.
- They hold office till reaching the age of retirement.
- Security of tenure
- Difficult procedure for removal of judges.
- The judiciary is not financially dependent on either the executive or legislature.
- Salaries and allowances of the judges are not subjected to the approval of the legislature.
- This gives the judiciary independence to adjudicate without fear of being criticised.

- The actions and decisions of the judges are immune from personal criticisms.
- The judiciary has the power to penalise those who are found guilty of contempt of court.
- This authority of the court is seen as an effective protection to the judges from unfair criticism.
- Parliament cannot discuss the conduct of the judges except when the proceeding to remove a judge is being carried out.

Importance of independence of the Supreme Court

- It is the final interpreter and guardian of the constitution.
- The Supreme Court is the guardian of the Fundamental Rights of the people.
- It is also the highest and final interpreter of the general law of the country.
- It is the highest court of appeal in civil and criminal matters.
- To maintain the Supremacy of the constitution there must be an impartial and independent authority to decide a dispute between Centre and States.
- In order for the judiciary as an institution to remain strong, it must be ensured that it is free from coercion and political influence.

Appointment and Removal of Judges

- Article 124 of the Indian Constitution
- It is mentioned in Article 124 that appointment by the President is to be done "after consultation" with judges of the Supreme Court, as the President may "deem necessary".
- Article 217, which deals with the appointment of High Court judges, says the President should consult the CJI, Governor, and Chief Justice of the High Court concerned.
- Further, the tenure of a CJI is until they attain the age of 65 years, while High Court judges retire at 62 years.

Appointment of the Chief Justice of India (CJI)

- Convention - the senior-most judge of the Supreme Court was appointed as the Chief Justice of India.

The above Convention was broken twice.

- In 1973 A. N. Ray was appointed as CJI superseding three senior Judges.
- Justice M.H. Beg was appointed superseding Justice H.R. Khanna (1975).

Appointment of Supreme Court Judges

Timeline for changes in the appointment procedures

1. Appointment of CJI 1950-1973
2. First judges case, 1982
3. Second judges case,1993
4. Third Judges Case, 1998
5. Collegium System
6. National Judicial Appointment Commission Act, 2014

Other Judges of the Supreme Court and the High Court
- Appointed by the President after 'consulting' the CJI.
- Final decisions in matters of appointment rested with the Council of Ministers.

Consultation with the Chief Justice?
- Supreme Court Observations (1982 – 1998)
- Initial Verdict - Role of the Chief Justice was purely consultative.
- 2nd verdict - Opinion of the Chief Justice must be followed by the President.
- "consultation" really meant "concurrence".

3RD VERDICT – COLLEGIUM SYSTEM
- Chief Justice should recommend names of persons to be appointed in consultation with four senior-most judges of the Court.
- Supreme Court has established the principle of collegiality in making recommendations for appointments.
- In judicial appointments, it is obligatory for the President to take into account the opinion of the CJI.
- The opinion of the CJI is binding on the Government.
- The opinion of the CJI must be formed after due consultation with a collegium of at least four senior-most judges of the Supreme Court.
- Even if two judges give an adverse opinion, then he should not send the recommendation to the Government.
- There are five members in the collegium system of India.

Executive v/s Judiciary
- 99th Constitutional Amendment Act, 2014 the National Judicial Commission Act (NJAC) to replace the collegium system for the appointment of judges
- NJAC was established to achieve greater transparency and accountability for the appointment of judges.
- But it was struck down by the Supreme Court on the grounds that it was against the "Independence of Judiciary" i.e Principles of Basic Structure since it involved the Political Executive in the appointment of Judges.

The current system of appointment of Supreme Court judges
- In judicial appointments, it is obligatory for the President to take into account the opinion of the CJI.
- The opinion of the CJI is binding on the Government.
- The opinion of the CJI must be formed after due consultation with a collegium of at least four senior-most judges of the Supreme Court.
- Even if two judges give an adverse opinion, then he should not send the recommendation to the Government.

- After the collegium's recommendations are finalised and received from the CJI, the Law Minister will put up the recommendation to the Prime Minister who will advise the President on the matter of appointment.

Removal of Judges

- Supreme Court/High Court judges Removal - very difficult procedure (general consensus among Member of Parliament required)
- Removal ground - ground of proven misbehaviour or incapacity.
- Motion – containing charges
- Passed by special Majority in both houses
- Executive role – in appointment of judges
- legislature role - in removal of judges
- both balance of power and independence of the judiciary -ensured

STRUCTURE OF JUDICIARY

- Single integrated judicial system.
- India does not have separate State courts.

Structure of the judiciary

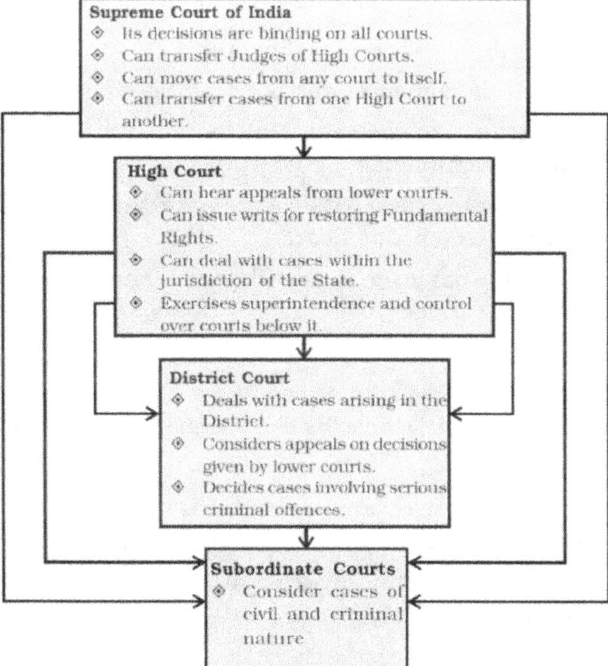

1. Supreme Court
2. High Courts
3. District and subordinate courts

The lower courts function under the direct superintendence of the higher courts.

Jurisdiction of Supreme Court

1. **Original Jurisdiction**
   - Cases that can be directly considered by the Supreme Court without going to the lower courts before that.
   - Cases involving federal relations go directly to the Supreme Court.
   - between the Union and the States and among the States
   - original jurisdiction - Supreme Court alone has the power to deal with such cases.
   - Supreme Court settles disputes
   - SC also interprets the powers of Union and State government as laid down in the Constitution.

2. **Writ Jurisdiction**
   - Any individual, whose fundamental right has been violated, can directly move the Supreme Court for remedy.
   - The Supreme Court can give special orders in the form of writs.(32)
   - The High Courts can also issue writs 9226)
   - Person can approach any court - SC/HC directly
   - Through such writs, the Court can give orders to the executive to act or not to act in a particular way.

3. **Appellate Jurisdiction**
   - The Supreme Court is the highest court of appeal.
   - A person can appeal to the Supreme Court against the decisions of the High Court.
   - High Court must certify that the case is fit for appeal.(involves a serious matter of interpretation of law or Constitution).
   - In criminal cases, if the lower court has sentenced a person to death then an appeal can be made to the High Court or Supreme Court.
   - Supreme Court holds the powers to decide whether to admit appeals even when appeal is not allowed by the High Court.
   - Appellate jurisdiction means that the Supreme Court will reconsider the case and the legal issues involved in it.
   - The High Courts too, have appellate jurisdiction over the decisions given by courts below them.

4. **Advisory Jurisdiction**
   - The President of India can refer any matter that is of public importance or that which involves interpretation of Constitution to Supreme Court for advice.
   - Supreme Court is not bound to give advice on such matters and the President is not bound to accept such an advice.

Judicial Activism

- Flourished in India through Public Interest Litigation (PIL) or Social Action Litigation (SAL).
- Judicial intervention for protection of existing rights, betterment of life conditions of the poor, protection of the environment, and many other issues in the interest of the public.
- PIL has become the most important vehicle of judicial activism.

- Through the PIL, the court has expanded the idea of rights.
- Clean air, unpolluted water, decent living, etc., are rights for the entire society.
- Individuals as parts of the society must have the right to seek justice wherever such rights were violated.
- Easy approach to courts
- Judiciary allowed public spirited citizens, social organisations and lawyers to file petitions on behalf of the needy and the deprived.

PIL (negative side)

- It has overburdened the courts.
- Judicial activism has blurred the line of distinction between the executive and legislature on the one hand and the judiciary on the other.
- The court has been involved in resolving questions which belong to the executive.
- reducing air or sound pollution or investigating cases of corruption or bringing about electoral reform is not exactly the duty of the Judiciary.
- These are matters to be handled by the administration under the supervision of the legislatures.
- Judicial activism has made the balance among the three organs of government very delicate.
- Democratic government is based on each organ of government respecting the powers and jurisdiction of the others

Judicial Review

- Most important power of the Supreme Court
- Review power - judiciary can interpret the Constitution and the laws passed by the legislature.
- To examine the constitutionality of any law
- if the law is inconsistent with the provisions of the Constitution - declared unconstitutional and inapplicable.
- Judicial review is nowhere mentioned in the Constitution.
- India has a written constitution and the Supreme Court can strike down a law that goes against fundamental rights, implicitly gives the Supreme Court the power of judicial review.
- If a central government makes a law, which according to some States, concerns a subject from the State list. – SC declare that unconstitutional
- Review Power of SC - power to review legislations on the ground that they violate fundamental rights or on the ground that they violate the federal distribution of powers.
- The review power extends to the laws passed by State legislatures also.
- Powerful Judiciary - writ + review
- PIL and judicial activism -made rights really meaningful for the poor and disadvantaged sections.

JUDICIARY AND PARLIAMENT

- Supreme Court actively involved in the administration of justice by giving directions to executive agencies.
- Indian Constitution -limited separation of powers and checks and balances.

- Each organ of the government has a clear area of functioning.
- Parliament is supreme in making laws and amending the Constitution
- Executive is supreme in implementing them
- Judiciary is supreme in settling disputes and deciding whether the laws that have been made are in accordance with the provisions of the Constitution.
- Despite such clear cut division of power the conflict between the Parliament and judiciary, and executive and the judiciary has remained a recurrent theme in Indian politics.

Right to property

- Differences emerged between the Parliament and the judiciary over right to property
- Parliament - restrictions on the right to hold property
- Reason – to implement land reforms
- Court - Parliament cannot thus restrict fundamental rights.
- Parliament - tried to amend the Constitution.
- Court - fundamental right cannot be abridged.

Parliament v/s Court

- Conflict period - 1967 to 1973
- Conflicting issues - land reform laws, laws enforcing preventive detention, laws governing reservations in jobs, regulations acquiring private property for public purposes

Kesavananda Bharati case (1973)

- Gave basic structure of the Constitution doctrine
- Court also stated that nobody—not even the Parliament (through amendment)—can violate the basic structure.

Court Verdict

- Right to property was not part of basic structure
- Court reserved to itself the right to decide whether various matters are part of the basic structure of the Constitution.

NATIONAL LEGAL SERVICES AUTHORITY OF INDIA (NALSA)

- It was formed on 9 November 1995 under the authority of the Legal Services Authorities Act 1987.
- Its purpose is to provide free legal services to eligible candidates and to organize Lok Adalats for speedy resolution of cases.
- The Chief Justice of India is patron-in-chief of NALSA while the second senior-most Judge of the Supreme Court of India is the Executive-Chairman.
- There is a provision for similar mechanism at state and district level also headed by Chief Justice of High Courts and Chief Judges of District courts respectively.
- The prime objective of NALSA is speedy disposal of cases and reducing the burden of judiciary.

12   Federalism

WHAT IS FEDERALISM?

Federalism

- Federalism is an institutional mechanism to accommodate two sets of polities—one at the regional level and the other at the national level.
- Each government is autonomous in its own sphere.
- In some federal countries, there is even a system of dual citizenship.
- India has only a single citizenship.
- Two sets of identities and loyalties—they belong to the region as well as the nation
- Gujaratis as well as Indians.
- Each level of the polity has distinct powers and responsibilities and has a separate system of government.
- The details of this dual system of government written in the constitution
- Constitution - source of the power of both sets of government.
- Division of Subjects
- Independent judiciary - To prevent conflicts between the centre and the State
- Real politics, culture, ideology and history determine the actual working of a federation.
- Political parties also determine the way a constitution would work.
- Single unit or State or linguistic group or ideology comes to dominate the entire federation it could generate a deep resentment among people or its units not sharing the dominant voice.
- These situations could lead to demands for secession by the aggrieved units or could even result in civil wars.

FEDERALISM IN THE INDIAN CONSTITUTION

- Even before Independence, most leaders of our national movement were aware that

This was clear at the time of Independence

- To govern a large country like India
- Necessary to divide the powers between provinces and the central government.
- Indian society had regional diversity and linguistic diversity.
- This diversity needed recognition.

- People of different regions and languages had to share power and in each region, people of that region should govern themselves.
- This was only logical if we wanted a democratic government.

What was not clear

- What should be the extent of powers to be enjoyed by the regional governments.
- Muslim League wanted greater representation to the Muslims

After Partition

- Constituent Assembly decided to frame a government that would be based on the principles of unity and cooperation between the centre and the States and separate powers to the States.
- The most important feature of the federal system adopted by the Indian Constitution is the principle that relations between the States and the centre would be based on cooperation.
- Thus, while recognising diversity, the Constitution emphasised unity.

Division of Powers - two sets of government created by the Indian Constitution

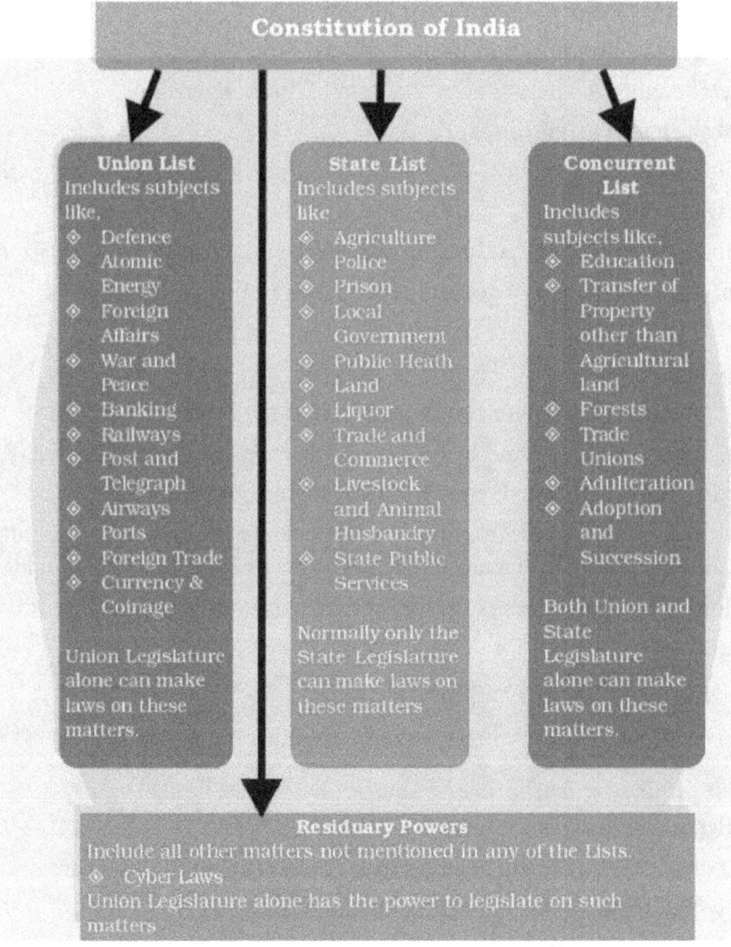

1. Union government (central government)
2. State government.

- Both of these have a constitutional status and clearly identified area of activity.
- If any dispute – it can be resolved by the Judiciary
- The Constitution clearly demarcates subjects, which are under the exclusive domain of the Union and those under the States.
- Economic and financial powers are centralised in the hands of the central government by the Constitution.
- The States have immense responsibilities but very meagre revenue sources.

FEDERALISM WITH A STRONG CENTRAL GOVERNMENT

Indian Constitution has created a strong Central Government

Reasons

- India is a country of continental dimensions with immense diversities and social problems.
- We required a federal constitution that would accommodate diversities.
- Strong centre to stem disintegration and bring about social and political change.
- During Independence – More than 500 princely states + provinces created by the British
- Integrated into existing States or new States had to be created.
- India's socio-economic problems needed to be handled by a strong central government in cooperation with the States.
- Poverty, illiteracy and inequalities of wealth were some of the problems that required planning and coordination.
- For Unity and Development - makers of the Constitution created a strong central government.

Important provisions that create a strong Central Government

- The very existence of a State including its territorial integrity is in the hands of Parliament.
- The Parliament is empowered to 'form a new State by separation of territory from any State or by uniting two or more States...'
- It can also alter the boundary of any State or even its name.
- The Constitution provides for some safeguards by way of securing the view of the concerned State legislature.

1. **Emergency provisions**
   - Can turn our federal polity into a highly centralised system
   - During an emergency, power becomes lawfully centralised.
   - Parliament also assumes the power to make laws on subjects within the jurisdiction of the States.
2. **Financial Powers**
   - Central government has very effective financial powers and responsibilities.
   - Items generating revenue are under the control of the central government.

- Central government has many revenue sources
- States are mostly dependent on the grants and financial assistance from the centre.
- India adopted rapid economic progress and development after independence which led to considerable centralisation of economic decision making.
- Union government uses its discretion to give grants and loans to States.

3. Governor Powers

- Governor has certain powers to recommend dismissal of the State government and the dissolution of the Assembly.
- Governor has the power to reserve a bill passed by the State legislature, for the assent of the President.
- This gives the central government an opportunity to delay the State legislation and also to examine such bills and veto them completely.
- If central government needs to legislate on matters from the State list. This is possible if the move is ratified by the Rajya Sabha.
- executive powers of the centre are superior to the executive powers of the States.

Article 257 (1)

- The executive power of every State shall be so exercised as not to impede or prejudice the exercise of the executive power of the Union, and the executive power of the Union shall extend to the giving of such directions to a State as may appear to the Government of India to be necessary for that purpose.

Integrated Administrative System.

- The all-India services are common to the entire territory of India and officers chosen for these services serve in the administration of the States.
- Thus, an IAS officer who becomes the collector or an IPS officer who serves as the Commissioner of Police, are under the control of the central government.
- States can neither take disciplinary action nor can they remove these officers from service.

Articles 33 and 34

- Parliament to protect persons in the service of the union or a state in respect of any action taken by them during martial law to maintain or restore order.
- This provisions further strengthens the powers of the union government.

  The Armed Forces Special Powers Act has been made on the basis of these provisions.
- This Act has created tensions between the people and the armed forces on some occasions.

CONFLICTS IN INDIA'S FEDERAL SYSTEM

- Constitution has vested very strong powers in the centre
- From time to time, States have demanded that they should be given more powers and more autonomy.

- This leads to tensions and conflicts in the relations between the centre and the States.
- Legal disputes Centre & State and States vs States resolved by the judiciary
- demands for autonomy - resolved through negotiations.

Centre-State Relations

- The Constitution is only a framework or a skeleton, its flesh and blood is provided by the actual processes of politics. Hence federalism

NATURE OF FEDERALISM IN INDIA

1950s and early 1960s – 1st phase of Federalism

- Foundation of Federalism - by Jawaharlal Nehru.
- Congress period
- dominance over the centre as well as the States.

In 1960s

- Congress dominance declined
- Role of regional parties
- demands for greater powers and greater autonomy to the States.
- different parties were ruling at the centre and in many States.
- This gave birth to a discussion about the concept of autonomy under a federal system.

1990s – 2nd Phase of Federalism in India

- Congress dominance ended / era of coalition politics especially at the centre.
- In the States too, different parties, both national and regional, have come to power.
- respect for diversity and the beginning of a more mature federalism.
- the issue of autonomy became very potent politically.

Demands for Autonomy Aspects

- More powers and important powers be assigned to the States.
- States should have independent sources of revenue and greater control over the resources - Financial autonomy.
- States resent the control of the centre over the administrative machinery.
- Autonomy demands may also be related to cultural and linguistic issues. Eg opposition to the domination of Hindi (in Tamil Nadu)

Role of Governors and President's Rule

- The Governor is not an elected office-holder.
- Governor is appointed by the central government
- Viewed as interference by the Central government in the functioning of the State government.

- When two different parties are in power at the centre and the State, the role of the Governor becomes even more controversial.
- Sarkaria Commission (1983 -1988) to examine the issues relating to centre-State relations, recommended that appointments of Governors should be strictly non-partisan.

Article 356

- Controversial article
- Provides for President's rule in any State.
- Government of the State cannot be carried on in accordance with the provisions of this Constitution.
- It results in the takeover of the State government by the Union government.
- The President's proclamation has to be ratified by Parliament.
- President's rule can be extended till three years.
- The Governor has the power to recommend the dismissal of the State government and suspension or dissolution of State assembly.
- Eg. State governments were dismissed even when they had a majority in the legislature. (Kerala in 1959)
- Supreme Court - Constitutional validity of the decision to impose President's rule can be examined by the judiciary.

After 1967

- Non-Congress governments in states
- Congress was in power at the centre.
- The centre has often used this provision to dismiss State governments

Demands for New States

- The national movement not only created a pan-Indian national unity; it also generated distinct unity around a common language, region and culture.
- It was decided that as far as possible, States would be created on the basis of common cultural and linguistic identity.
- This ultimately led to the demand for the creation of linguistic States after Independence.
- States Reorganisation Commission - 1953
- Recommended the creation of linguistic States
- In 1956, reorganisation of some States took place.
- Beginning of the creation of linguistic States
- Gujarat and Maharashtra were created in 1960
- Punjab and Haryana were separated from each other in 1966.
- North Eastern region was reorganised and new States like Manipur, Tripura, Meghalaya, Mizoram and Arunachal Pradesh were created.

In 2000

- Some of the larger States were further divided
- need for greater administrative efficiency.
- Thus Madhya Pradesh, Uttar Pradesh and Bihar were divided to create three new States.
- They are: Chhattisgarh, Uttarakhand and Jharkhand respectively.
- In 2014, the State of Telangana was formed by dividing Andhra Pradesh.
- Some regions and linguistic groups are still struggling for separate Statehood like Vidarbha in Maharashtra.

Interstate Conflicts

- Centre v/s State – fighting over autonomy , share in revenue resources
- State v/s State - disputes between two States or among more than two States.
- Dispute (if legal in nature) resolved by judiciary
- Dispute (political) - resolved only through negotiations and mutual understanding.

Dispute Types

Border dispute

- States have certain claims over territories belonging to neighbouring States.

Eg. of border disputes

- Maharashtra and Karnataka over the city of Belgaum.
- Manipur and Nagaland
- Punjab and Haryana over Chandigarh

Sharing of river waters

- Cauvery water dispute - between Tamil Nadu and Karnataka.
- Farmers in both the States are dependent on Cauvery waters.
- Gujarat, Madhya Pradesh and Maharashtra are battling over sharing the waters of Narmada river.

Special provisions to some states

- Constitution has some special provisions for some States given their peculiar social and historical circumstances.
- Most of the special provisions pertain to the north eastern States (Assam, Nagaland, Arunachal Pradesh, Mizoram, etc.) largely due to their sizeable indigenous tribal population with a distinct history and culture.
- Special provisions also exist for hilly States like Himachal Pradesh and some other States like Andhra Pradesh, Goa, Gujarat, Maharashtra Sikkim and Telangana.

Article 370

- Concurrence of the State was required for making any laws in matters mentioned in the Union and Concurrent lists.

- In the case of Jammu and Kashmir, the central government had only limited powers and other powers listed in the Union list and Concurrent list could be used only with the consent of the State government.
- This gave greater autonomy to the State of Jammu and Kashmir.
- J&K had a separate constitution and a flag
- No emergency due to internal disturbances could be declared in J&K without the concurrence of the State.
- The Union government could not impose a financial emergency in the State and the Directive Principles did not apply in J&K.
- Amendments to the Indian Constitution (under Art. 368) could apply in concurrence with the government of J&K.
- At present, the special status given under 370 no longer exists.
- By the Jammu and Kashmir reorganisation Act 2019, the State has been bifurcated into two Union Territories viz., (i) Jammu and Kashmir and (ii) Ladakh.
- The new arrangement has come into effect from 31 October, 2019.

Present Status of Jammu and Kashmir

The abrogation of Article 370 to end the special status of Jammu and Kashmir

- With a resolution and a bill, the Central government scripted a historical change in the status of Jammu and Kashmir
- On August 5, 2019, Union Home Minister Amit Shah introduced a proposal in Parliament for ending the special status of Jammu and Kashmir and its bifurcation into two Union Territories.
- Jammu and Kashmir had a special status granted under Article 370 and Article 35A (created through a Presidential Order) of the Constitution

Jammu and Kashmir Reorganisation Act, 2019

- It is an act by the Indian Parliament where the State of Jammu and Kashmir was bifurcated into two union territories — Jammu & Kashmir and Ladakh.
- The Union Territory of Jammu and Kashmir has a legislative assembly
- The L-G will have the power to dissolve the Jammu and Kashmir Legislative Assembly.
- The Union Territory of Ladakh does not have a legislative assembly and is administered by the Lieutenant Governor alone.
- The Union Territory of Ladakh will include the districts Leh and Kargil
- Out of the six Lok Sabha seats in the state of Jammu and Kashmir, five remained with the Union Territory of Jammu and Kashmir and one went to the Union Territory of Ladakh.

13 Local Government in India

WHAT IS LOCAL GOVERNMENT

- Local government is government at the village and district level.
- Constitutional status was accorded to local government institutions in 1993.

WHY LOCAL GOVERNMENTS?

- To look after local affairs
- Involves in the day-to-day life and problems of ordinary citizens.
- local knowledge and local interest - essential ingredients for democratic decision making.
- local government is so near the common people.
- convenient for the people to approach the local government for solving their problems
- effective in protecting the local interests of the people.
- active participation and purposeful accountability
- In a democracy, tasks, which can be performed locally, should be left in the hands of the local people and their representatives.

Growth Of Local Government In India

Earlier time

- Self-governing village communities – Sabhas (village assemblies).
- Took the shape of Panchayats (an assembly of five persons)

Modern times

- Elected local government bodies were created after 1882 - Lord Rippon
- Government of India Act 1919, village panchayats were established in a number of provinces. This trend continued after the Government of India Act of 1935.

Mahatma Gandhi view on Local bodies

- Strongly pleaded for decentralisation of economic and political power.
- Strengthening village panchayats was a means of effective decentralisation.
- Panchayats - instruments of decentralisation and participatory democracy.

Local government

- Subject of local government was assigned to the States.
- It was also mentioned in the Directive Principles as one of the policy directives to all governments in the country - non-justiciable and primarily advisory in its nature.
- did not receive adequate importance in the Constitution.

Reasons

- turmoil due to the Partition resulted in a strong unitary inclination in the Constitution.
- extreme localism as a threat to unity and integration of the nation.
- faction and caste-ridden nature of rural society
- factionalism

Efforts in the direction of developing local government bodies (events before the Constitutional amendment)

- Community Development Programme in 1952 - promote people's participation in local development in a range of activities.
- A three-tier Panchayati Raj system of local government was recommended for the rural areas.
- Some States (like Gujarat, Maharashtra) adopted the system of elected local bodies around 1960.
- But did not have enough powers and functions to look after the local development.
- dependent on the State and central governments for financial assistance
- In 1989 the P.K.Thungon Committee recommended constitutional recognition for the local government bodies

73rd and 74th Amendments

- Introduced in – 1989
- Aim - strengthening local governments and ensuring an element of uniformity in their structure and functioning across the country.
- In 1992, the 73rd and 74th constitutional amendments were passed by the Parliament.
- The 73rd Amendment is about rural local governments (which are also known as Panchayati Raj Institutions or PRIs) and the 74th amendment made the provisions relating to urban local government (Nagarpalikas).
- The 73rd and 74th Amendments came into force in 1993.
- States were given one year's time for making necessary changes in their respective State laws

73rd Amendment

Three Tier Structure

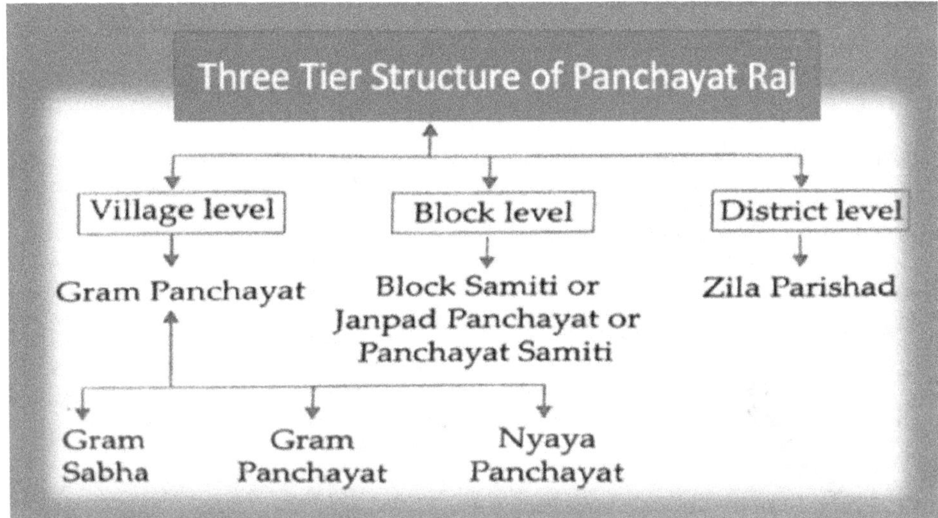

1. **Village Level - Gram Panchayat**
   - At the base
   - covers a village or group of villages.
2. **Block Level - Intermediary level/Mandal//taluka**
   - The intermediary level is the Mandal (also referred to as Block or Taluka).
   - These bodies are called Mandal or Taluka Panchayats.
   - Intermediary level body need not be constituted in smaller States.
3. **District Level - Zilla Parishad**
   - At the apex is the Zilla Panchayat/Parishad covering the entire rural area of the District.

Gram Sabha
- The amendment also made a provision for the mandatory creation of the Gram Sabha.
- The Gram Sabha would comprise all the adult members registered as voters in the Panchayat area.
- Its role and functions are decided by State legislation.

Elections to Panchayats
- All the three levels of Panchayati Raj institutions are elected directly by the people.
- The term of each Panchayat body is five years.
- If the State government dissolves the Panchayat before the end of its five year term, fresh elections must be held within six months of such dissolution.

Reservations

- One third of the positions in all panchayat institutions are reserved for women.
- Reservations for Scheduled Castes and Scheduled Tribes are also provided for at all the three levels, in proportion to their population.
- If the States find it necessary, they can also provide for reservations for the other backward classes (OBCs).
- Reservations apply to ordinary members and positions of Chairpersons at all the three levels. Reservation of one-third of the seats for women general category seats reserved for Scheduled Castes, Scheduled Tribes and backward castes.

Transfer of Subjects

- Twenty-nine subjects
- earlier in the State list of subjects
- Now listed in the Eleventh Schedule of the Constitution.
- These subjects are to be transferred to the Panchayati Raj institutions.
- transfer depends upon the State legislation.

Adivasi Population

- The provisions of the 73rd amendment were not made applicable to the areas inhabited by the Adivasi populations in many States of India.
- In 1996, a separate act was passed extending the provisions of the Panchayat system to these areas.
- Adivasi communities - traditional customs of managing common resources such as forests and small water reservoirs, etc.
- new act protects the rights of these communities to manage their resources in ways acceptable to them.
- more powers are given to the Gram Sabhas of these areas and elected village panchayats have to get the consent of the Gram Sabha in many respects.

State Election Commissioners

- Responsible for conducting elections to the Panchayati Raj institutions.
- Office of the State Election Commissioner is autonomous like the Election Commissioner of India.
- The State Election Commissioner is an independent officer and is not linked to nor is this officer under the control of the Election Commission of India.

State Finance Commission

- State government to appoint a State Finance Commission once in five years.
- To examine the financial position of the local governments in the State.
- It would also review the distribution of revenues between the State and local governments / between rural and urban local governments

74th Amendment - Urban local bodies or Nagarpalikas.

Urban Area

- a minimum population of 5,000;
- at least 75 per cent of male working population engaged in non-agricultural occupations and
- a density of population of at least 400 persons per sq. km.
- As per the 2011 Census, about 31% of India's population lives in urban areas.
- All the provisions of the 73rd amendment are incorporated in the 74th amendment
- Constitution mandated the transfer of a list of functions from the State government to the urban local bodies.
- These functions have been listed in the Twelfth Schedule of the Constitution.

IMPLEMENTATION OF 73RD AND 74TH AMENDMENTS

- All States have now passed a legislation to implement the provisions of the 73rd and 74th amendments.
- The 73rd and 74th amendments have created uniformity in the structures of Panchayati Raj and Nagarpalika institutions across the country.
- Reservation for women at the Panchayats and Nagarpalikas has ensured the presence of a significant number of women in local bodies. As this reservation is also applicable for the positions of Sarpanch and Adhyaksha, a large number of women elected representatives have come to occupy these positions. There are at least 200 women Adhyakshas in Zilla Panchayats, another 2000 women who are Presidents of the block or taluka panchayats and more than 80,000 women Sarpanchas in Gram Panchayats. bodies. In many cases, women were unable to assert their presence or were mere proxies for the male members of their family who sponsored their election. Such instances, however are becoming fewer.
- The provision for reservation for women at the Panchayats and Nagarpalikas has ensured the presence of a significant number of women in local bodies. As this reservation is also applicable for the positions of Sarpanch and Adhyaksha, a large number of women elected representatives have come to occupy these positions. There are at least 200 women Adhyakshas in Zilla Panchayats, another 2000 women who are Presidents of the block or taluka panchayats and more than 80,000 women Sarpanchas in Gram Panchayats.

14 Our Constitution

INDIAN CONSTITUTION

* Framework within which the government of our country operates.
* adopted on 26 November 1949.
* Its implementation formally started from 26 January 1950.
* Continues to function

HOW TO AMEND THE CONSTITUTION?

Article 368:

...Parliament may in exercise of its constituent power amend by way of addition, variation or repeal any provision of this Constitution in accordance with the procedure laid down in this article.

Constitution – a combination of flexibility and Rigidity

* Constitution must be amended if so required.
* But it must be protected from unnecessary and frequent changes.
* Constitution to be 'flexible' and at the same time 'rigid'.
* Flexible means open to changes and rigid means resistant to changes.
* A constitution that can be very easily changed or modified is often called flexible.
* In the case of constitutions, which are very difficult to amend, they are described as rigid.
* The Indian Constitution combines both these characteristics.

Constitutional makers thoughts of flexibility

* aware that there may be some faults or mistakes in the Constitution
* Constitution could not be totally free of errors.
* Whenever such mistakes would come to light – it can easily amended

Constitutional makers thoughts on Rigidity

* Strong centre

- Constitution was framing a federal polity
- The rights and powers of the States could not be changed without the consent of the States.
- Tough process of amendment

Two methods

1. Amendment can be made by special majority of the two houses of the Parliament.
2. It requires special majority of the Parliament and consent of half of the State legislatures.

All amendments to the Constitution are initiated only in the Parliament.

- Besides the special majority in the Parliament no outside agency— —like a constitution commission or a separate body—is required for amending the Constitution.
- No referendum is required for ratification of the amendment.
- An amendment bill, like all other bills, goes to the President for his assent, but in this case, the President has no powers to send it back for reconsideration.
- These details show how rigid and complicated the amending process could have been.
- Our Constitution avoids these complications. This makes the amendment procedure relatively simple. But more importantly, this process underlines an important principle: only elected representatives of the people are empowered to consider and take final decisions on the question of amendments. Thus, sovereignty of elected representatives (parliamentary sovereignty) is the basis of the amendment procedure.

Ratification by States

- When an amendment aims to modify an article related to distribution of powers between the States and the central government, or articles related to representation, it is necessary that the States must be consulted and that they give their consent.
- Federalism means that powers of the States must not be at the mercy of the central government.
- The Constitution has ensured this by providing that legislatures of half the States have to pass the amendment bill before the amendment comes into effect.
- For some parts of the Constitution, greater or wider consensus in the polity is expected.
- This provision also respects the States and gives them participation in the process of amendment.
- At the same time, care is taken to keep this procedure somewhat flexible even in its more rigid format: consent of only half the States is required and simple majority of the State legislature is sufficient.
- Thus, the amendment process is not impracticable even after taking into consideration this more stringent condition.
- Constitution of India can be amended through large-scale consensus and limited participation of the States.

- The founding fathers took care that Constitution would not be open to easy tampering. And yet, future generations were given the right to amend and modify according to the needs and requirements of the time.

BASIC STRUCTURE AND EVOLUTION OF THE CONSTITUTION

Kesavananda Bharati case contributed to the evolution of the Constitution in the following ways:

- It has set specific limits to Parliament's power to amend the Constitution.

- It says that no amendment can violate the basic structure of the Constitution

- It allows Parliament to amend any and all parts of the Constitution (within this limitation)

- It places the Judiciary as the final authority in deciding if an amendment violates basic structure and what constitutes the basic structure.

- The Supreme Court gave the Kesavananda ruling in 1973

- In the past four decades, this decision has governed all interpretations of the Constitution and all institutions in the country have accepted the theory of basic structure.

- In fact, the theory of basic structure is itself an example of a living constitution.

- There is no mention of this theory in the Constitution.

- It has emerged from judicial interpretation.

- Thus, the Judiciary and its interpretation have practically amended the Constitution without a formal amendment.

- All living documents evolve in this manner through debates, arguments, competition and practical politics.

- Since 1973, the Court has, in many cases, elaborated upon this theory of basic structure and given instances of what constitutes the basic structure of the Constitution of India. In a sense, the basic structure doctrine has further consolidated the balance between rigidity and flexibility: by saying that certain parts cannot be amended, it has underlined the rigid nature while by allowing amendments to all others it has underlined the flexible nature of the amending process.

JUDICIAL CONTRIBUTION TO THE EVOLUTION OF THE CONSTITUTION

- There are many other examples of how judicial interpretation changed our understanding of the Constitution.

- In many decisions the Supreme Court had held that reservations in jobs and educational institutions cannot exceed fifty per cent of the total seats.

- This has now become an accepted principle.

- Similarly, in the case involving reservations for other backward classes, the Supreme Court introduced the idea of creamy layer and ruled that persons belonging to this category were not entitled to benefits under reservations.

- In the same manner, the Judiciary has contributed to an informal amendment by interpreting various provisions concerning right to education, right to life and liberty and the right to form and manage minority educational institutions. These are instances of how rulings by the Court contribute to the evolution of the Constitution.

IMPORTANT AMENDMENTS TO INDIAN CONSTITUTION

1st Amendment, 1950

Amend Articles/Schedules

- 15, 19, 85, 87, 174, 176, 341, 342, 372 and 376.
- Insert articles 31A and 31B
- Insert schedule 9.

Provisions

- Three more reasons for restricting freedom of speech and expression have been added: public order, friendly relations with foreign states, and incitement to an offence.
- It also made the restrictions 'reasonable' and, therefore, in nature, justiciable.
- Right to practice any profession or to carry on any trade or business as contained in Article 19 of the Constitution
- The Ninth Schedule along with Articles 31A and 31B were inserted in the Constitution to protect laws, such as the land reform and other laws, from being challenged in the courts on the ground of violation of fundamental rights.

7th Amendment, 1956

Amend articles/schedules

- 1, 3, 49, 80, 81, 82, 131, 153, 158, 168, 170, 171, 216, 217, 220, 222, 224, 230, 231 and 232.
- Insert articles 258A, 290A, 298, 350A, 350B, 371, 372A and 378A.
- Amend part 8.
- Amend schedules 1, 2, 4 and 7.

Provisions

- Reorganisation of states on linguistic lines
- Abolition of Class A, B, C, D states
- Introduction of Union territories.
- States reorganized into 14 states and 6 federal territories.
- Establishment of new High Courts, High Court Judges etc.

10th Amendment, 1961

- Amend article 240.
- Amend schedule 1.

Provisions

- Incorporation of Dadra and Nagar Haveli as a Union Territory, consequent to acquisition from Portugal.

11th Amendment, 1961

- Amend articles 66 and 71.
- Proposed that election of President or Vice President could not be challenged on the ground of any vacancy in the appropriate electoral college.

12th Amendment, 1962

- Amend article 240 and Amend schedule 1
- Included Goa, Daman and Diu as a Union Territory and to amend Article 240 for the purpose.

13th Amendment, 1962

- Amend article 170.
- Insert new article 371A.
- Nagaland was formed with an agreement between Government of India and Naga People's Convention.

14th Amendment, 1962

- Amend articles 81 and 240.
- Insert article 239A.
- Amend schedules 1 and 4
- Pondicherry was included in the First Schedule as a Union Territory
- Creation of Legislature by Parliamentary law for Himachal Pradesh, Manipur, Tripura, Goa, Daman and Diu and Pondicherry

22nd Amendment, 1969

- Amend article 275.
- Insert articles 244A and 371B
- New autonomous state of Meghalaya with in the state of Assam.

24th Amendment, 1971

- Amend articles 13 and 368.
- Removed all doubts regarding the power of Parliament to amend the Constitution including the Fundamental Rights.
- Enable parliament to dilute fundamental rights through amendments to the constitution
- The President's assent to Constitutional Amendment Bill was made compulsory

25th Amendment Act, 1971

- Fundamental Right to Property was curtailed

26th Amendment Act 1971

- Amend article 366.
- Insert article 363A.
- Remove articles 291 and 362.
- Abolition of privy purse paid to former rulers of princely states which were incorporated into the Indian Republic.

31st Amendment, 1973

- Amend articles 81, 330 and 332.
- Increase size of Parliament from 525 to 545 seats.
- Reduced the upper limit for the representation of union territories from 25 members to 20.

35th Amendment, 1974

- Amend articles 80 and 81.
- Insert article 2A.
- Insert schedule 10.
- Conferred Sikkim the status of an associate State of Indian Union.

36th Amendment, 1975

- Amend articles 80 and 81.
- Insert article 371F.
- Amend schedules 1 and 4.
- Made Sikkim a full-fledged State of Indian Union and to include it in the First Schedule to the Constitution

40th Amendment Act, 1976

- Parliament was empowered to specify from time to time the limits of the territorial waters, the continental shelf, the exclusive economic zone (EEZ) and the maritime zones of India.

42nd Amendment, 1976

- Amend articles 31, 31C, 39, 55, 74, 77, 81, 82, 83, 100, 102, 103, 105, 118, 145, 150, 166, 170, 172, 189, 191, 192, 194, 208, 217, 225, 226, 227, 228, 311, 312, 330, 352, 353, 356, 357, 358, 359, 366, 368 and 371F.
- Insert articles 31D, 32A, 39A, 43A, 48A, 131A, 139A, 144A, 226A, 228A and 257A.
- Insert parts 4A and 14A.
- Amend schedule 7.
- Amendment passed during internal emergency

- Provides for curtailment of fundamental rights, imposes fundamental duties and changes to the basic structure of the constitution by making India a "Sovereign Socialist Secular Democratic Republic".
- The Supreme Court, in Minerva Mills v. Union of India, quashed the amendments to Articles 31C and 368 as it was in contravention with the basic structure of the Constitution.
- Ideals of socialism, secularism and the integrity of the nation were adopted
- Directive Principles were given precedence over Fundamental Rights
- Inserted a new chapter on the Fundamental Duties of citizens

44th Amendment, 1978

- Amend articles 19, 22, 30, 31A, 31C, 38, 71, 74, 77, 83, 103, 105, 123, 132, 133, 134, 139A, 150, 166, 172, 192, 194, 213, 217, 225, 226, 227, 239B, 329, 352, 356, 358, 359, 360 and 371F.
- Insert articles 134A and 361A.
- Remove articles 31, 257A and 329A.
- Amend part 12.
- Amend schedule 9.
- Amendment passed after revocation of internal emergency in the Country.
- Right to property from the list of fundamental rights and made it a legal right
- Provided "armed rebellion" as one of the circumstances for declaration of emergency

52nd Amendment, 1985

- Amend articles 101, 102, 190 and 191.
- Insert schedule 10.
- Suitable provisions were made with respect to splits in and merger of political parties.
- Anti Defection Law – Provide disqualification of members from parliament and assembly in case of defection from one party to other.
- However, parts of the 10th Schedule to the Constitution of India was struck down by the Supreme Court in the case of Kihoto Hollohan v. Zachillhu 1992 SCR (1) 686, for being in contravention with Article 368 of the Constitution.

53rd Amendment, 1986

- Insert article 371G.
- Mostly revolved around the state of Mizoram.

55th Amendment, 1986

- Insert article 371H
- Conferred statehood on the Union Territory of Arunachal Pradesh

56th Amendment, 1987

- Insert article 371I.
- Union Territory of Daman and Diu and the formation of the state of Goa.

61st Amendment, 1989

- Amend article 326
- Reduction of the voting age from 21 to 18 years by amending Article 326

65th Amendment, 1989

- Amend article 338.
- National Commission for Scheduled Castes and Scheduled Tribes formed and its statutory powers specified in The Constitution.

66th Amendment, 1990

- Amend schedule 9
- Place land reform acts and amendments to these act under Schedule 9 of the constitution
- Andhra Pradesh, Bihar, Gujarat, Himachal Pradesh,Karnataka, Kerala, Madhya Pradesh, Maharashtra, Orissa, Rajasthan, TamilNadu, Uttar Pradesh, West Bengal and administration of the Union Territory of Puducherry were added to the Ninth Schedule
- Relating to land reforms and ceiling on agricultural land holdings)

69th Amendment, 1991

- Insert articles 239AA and 239AB.
- Union territory of Delhi was renamed as the National Capital Territory of Delhi

70th Amendment, 1992

- Amend articles 54 and 239AA.
- Included the elected members of the legislative assemblies of union territories (National Capital Territory of Delhi and Union Territory of Pondicherry) in the electoral college for the election of the President under Article 54 of the Constitution.

71st Amendment, 1992

- Amend schedule 8
- Included Konkani, Manipuri and Nepali languages in the Eighth Schedule to the Constitution.

73rd Amendment, 1993

- Insert part 9. Insert schedule 11.
- A new Part-IX and 11th Schedule were added in the Indian Constitution to recognize Panchayati Raj Institutions and provisions related to them
- Gave constitutional status to the Panchayati Raj Institutions

74th Amendment, 1993

- Insert part 9A , insert schedule 12 , amend article 280.
- A new Part IX-A and 12th Schedule were added to the Indian Constitution
- Provisions for local administrative bodies in urban areas such as towns and cities were added.

86th Amendment, 2002

- Amend articles 45 and 51A.
- Insert article 21A.
- Article 21A deals with Right to Education that "the State shall provide free and compulsory education to all children of the age of six to fourteen years"
- A new Fundamental Duty under Article 51 A was added – "It shall be the duty of every citizen of India who is a parent or guardian to provide opportunities for education to his child or ward between the age of six and fourteen years"

87th Amendment, 2003

- Amend articles 81, 82, 170 and 330.
- 2001 national census population figures were to be used for state-wise distribution of parliamentary seats.

89th Amendment, 2003

- Amend article 338.
- Insert article 338A.
- The National Commission for Scheduled Castes and Scheduled Tribes was bifurcated into The National Commission for Scheduled Castes and The National Commission for Scheduled Tribes.

91st Amendment, 2003

- Amend articles 75 and 164.
- Insert article 361B.
- Amend schedule 10.
- Restricts the size of the Council of Ministers in the Union Government and in a State Government to fifteen percent of the total number of legislative members.

92st Amendment, 2003

- Amend schedule 8.
- Bodo, Dogri, Santali and Maithali were added as official languages to the 8th Schedule
- Total official languages were increased from 18 to 22

94th Amendment, 2006

- Amend article 164.
- To provide for a Minister of Tribal Welfare in newly created Jharkhand and Chhattisgarh States including Madhya Pradesh and Orissa.

97th Amendment, 2012

- Amend Art 19 and added Art 43B and Part IXB
- Co-operative Societies were granted constitutional status
- Right to form cooperative societies made a fundamental right (Article 19)
- A new Directive Principle of State Policy (Article 43-B) to promote cooperative societies
- A new part IX-B was added in the constitution for cooperative societies
- Added the words "or co-operative societies" after the word "or unions" in Article 19(l)(c) and insertion of article 43B i.e., Promotion of Co-operative Societies and added Part-IXB i.e., The Co-operative Societies.
- In July 2021 Supreme Court Struck Part of the amendment as it was not ratified by the states.

99th Amendment, 2012

- Insertion of new articles 124A, 124B and 124C. Amendments to Articles 127, 128, 217, 222, 224A, 231.
- Formation of a National Judicial Appointments Commission.
- The amendment was struck down by the Supreme Court on 16 October 2015.

100th Amendment, 2015

- Amendment of First Schedule to Constitution
- Exchange of certain enclave territories with Bangladesh and conferment of citizenship rights to residents of enclaves consequent to signing of Land Boundary Agreement (LBA) Treaty between India and Bangladesh.

101st Amendment, 2017

- Introduction of "The Goods and Services Tax (GST)" and provision of compensation to states for loss of revenue on account of introduction of goods and services tax. Addition of articles 246A, 269A, 279A. Deletion of Article 268A.
- Amendment of articles 248, 249, 250, 268, 269, 270, 271, 286, 366, 368, Sixth Schedule, Seventh Schedule.

102nd Amendment, 2018

- Constitutional status to National Commission for Backward Classes.
- Addition of articles 338B, 342A, and Added Clause 26C.Modification of articles 338, 366

103rd Amendment, 2019

- A maximum of 10% Reservation for Economically Weaker Sections (EWSs) of citizens of classes other than the classes mentioned in clauses (4) and (5) of Article 15, i.e. Classes other than socially and educationally backward classes of citizens or the Scheduled Castes and the Scheduled Tribes.

- Inserted Clause [6] under Article 15 as well as Inserted Clause [6] under Article 16.

104th Amendment, 2020

- To extend the reservation of seats for SCs and STs in the Lok Sabha and states assemblies from Seventy years to Eighty years. Removed the reserved seats for the Anglo-Indian community in the Lok Sabha and state assemblies.

- Amend article 334.

105th Amendment, 2021

- Amended Article 338B, 342A and 366

- To designed to clarify that the states can maintain the "state list" of OBCs.

- To restore the power of the state governments to identify Other Backward Classes (OBCs) that are socially and educationally backward.

- This amendment annulled the Supreme Court judgement of 11 May 2021, which had empowered only the Central government for such identification.

15 Philosophy Of The Constitution

WHAT IS MEANT BY PHILOSOPHY OF THE CONSTITUTION?

Constitution consists of laws/ can only have a legalistic values, not a political philosophy approach

But

- It is true that all laws do not have a moral content, but many laws are closely connected to our deeply held values.

How ?

- Law prohibit discrimination of persons on grounds of language or religion.
- It is connected to the idea of equality.
- Such a law exists because we value equality.
- Therefore, there is a connection between laws and moral values.

Constitution

- As a document that is based on a certain moral vision.
- We need to adopt a political philosophy approach to the constitution.

POLITICAL PHILOSOPHY APPROACH TO THE CONSTITUTION

- Conceptual structure of the constitution - meanings of terms used in the constitution such as 'rights', 'citizenship', 'minority' or 'democracy'?
- Coherent vision of society and polity conditional upon an interpretation of the key concepts of the constitution.
- Constitution must be read in conjunction with the Constituent Assembly Debates
- The justification of values embedded in the Constitution - set of reasons
- Needed to find out the moral content expressed in it
- to use it to arbitrate between varying interpretations of the many core values in our polity.

WHAT IS THE POLITICAL PHILOSOPHY OF OUR CONSTITUTION?

- It is hard to describe this philosophy in one word.
- It is liberal, democratic, egalitarian, secular, and federal, open to community values, sensitive to the needs of religious and linguistic minorities as well as historically disadvantaged groups, and committed to building a common national identity.
- It is committed to freedom, equality, social justice, and some form of national unity.
- There is a clear emphasis on peaceful and democratic measures for putting this philosophy into practice.

INDIVIDUAL FREEDOM

- Constitution commitment to individual freedom.
- This commitment did not emerge miraculously out of calm deliberations around a table.
- It was the product of continuous intellectual and political activity of well over a century.

OTHER INTELLECTUAL AND POLITICAL ACTIVITY

- Freedom of expression is an integral part of the Indian Constitution.
- It is the freedom from arbitrary arrest.
- In Rowlatt Act - opposed so vehemently/sought to deny this basic freedom.
- Other individual freedoms such as freedom of conscience are part of the liberal ideology.
- Indian Constitution has a pretty strong liberal character.
- Fundamental rights chapter - Constitution values individual freedom.
- Before the adoption of the Constitution, every single resolution, scheme, bill and report of the Indian National Congress mentioned individual rights

SOCIAL JUSTICE

- Indian Constitution is liberal
- It is liberal only in the classical western sense
- Classical liberalism always privileges rights of the individuals over demands of social justice and community values.

LIBERALISM OF THE INDIAN CONSTITUTION

- It was always linked to social justice.
- Eg - provision for reservations for Scheduled Castes and Scheduled Tribes in the Constitution.
- mere granting of the right to equality was not enough to overcome age-old injustices suffered by these groups or to give real meaning to their right to vote.
- Special constitutional measures were required to advance their interests.
- Therefore the constitution makers provided a number of special measures to protect the interests of Scheduled Castes and Scheduled Tribes such as the reservation of seats in legislatures.

- The Constitution also made it possible for the government to reserve public sector jobs for these groups.

RESPECT FOR DIVERSITY AND MINORITY RIGHTS

- The Indian Constitution encourages equal respect between communities.
- This was not easy in our country,
- First because communities do not always have a relationship of equality; they tend to have hierarchical relationships with one another (as in the case of caste).
- Second, when these communities do see each other as equals, they also tend to become rivals (as in the case of religious communities).

INDIAN CONTEXT

- we have more openly acknowledged the value of communities.
- India is a land of multiple cultural communities.
- Unlike Germany or France we have several linguistic and religious communities.
- It was important to ensure that no one community systematically dominates others.
- This made it mandatory for our Constitution to recognise community based rights.
- One such right is the right of religious communities to establish and run their own educational institutions.
- Such institutions may receive money from the government.

SECULARISM : WESTERN CONCEPT

- Western conception, of secularism means mutual exclusion of state and religion in order to protect values such as individual freedom and citizenship rights of individuals.

Mutual exclusion

- both religion and state must stay away from the internal affairs of one another.
- The state must not intervene in the domain of religion
- religion likewise should not dictate state policy or influence the conduct of the state.
- religion and state must be strictly separated.

Strict separation – why?

- It is to safeguard the freedom of individuals.
- States which lend support to organised religions make them more powerful than they already are.
- Religious organisations start dictating how they should relate to God or how they should pray.
- To protect religious freedom of individuals, state must not help religious organisations.

- But at the same time, state should not tell religious organisations how to manage their affairs.
- States should neither help nor hinder religions.
- Instead, they should keep themselves at an arm's length from them.
- This has been the prevalent western conception of secularism.

Indian Concept

- The makers of the Constitution had work out an alternative conception of secularism.
- They departed from the western model in two ways and for two different reasons.

Rights of Religious Groups

- They recognised that inter- community equality was as necessary as equality between individuals.
- A person's freedom and sense of self-respect was directly dependent upon the status of her community.
- If one community was dominated by another, then its members would also be significantly less free.
- If, on the other hand, their relations were equal, marked by an absence of domination, then its members would also walk about with dignity, self-respect and freedom.
- Thus, the Indian Constitution grants rights to all religious communities such as the right to establish and maintain their educational institutions.
- Freedom of religion in India means the freedom of religion of both individuals and communities.

State's Power of Intervention

- Separation in India could not mean mutual exclusion.
- Religiously sanctioned customs such as untouchability deprived individuals of the most basic dignity and self-respect.
- Such customs were so deeply rooted and pervasive that without active state intervention, there was no hope of their dissolution.
- The state simply had to interfere in the affairs of religion. Such intervention was not always negative.
- The state could also help religious communities by giving aid to educational institutions run by them.
- The state may help or hinder religious communities depending on which mode of action promotes values such as freedom and equality.
- In India separation between religion and state did not mean their mutual exclusion but rather principled distance

Principled distance

- Idea that allows the state to be distant from all religions so that it can intervene or abstain from interference, depending upon which of these two would better promote liberty, equality and social justice.

THREE CORE FEATURES OF OUR CONSTITUTION

- First, our Constitution reinforces and reinvents forms of liberal individualism.
- Second, our Constitution upholds the principle of social justice without compromising on individual liberties.
- Third, against the background of inter-communal strife, the Constitution upholds its commitment to group rights (the right to the expression of cultural particularity). This indicates that the framers of the Constitution were more than willing to face the challenges of what more than four decades later has come to be known as multiculturalism.

UNIVERSAL FRANCHISE

- Regarded as achievements
- Perception - traditional hierarchies in India are congealed and more or less impossible to eliminate
- The right to vote has only recently been extended to women and to the working class in stable, Western democracies.
- Once the idea of a nation took root among the elite, the idea of democratic self-government followed.
- Indian nationalism always conceived of a political order based on the will of every single member of society.
- The idea of universal franchise lay securely within the heart of nationalism.
- As early as the Constitution of India Bill (1895), the first non-official attempt at drafting a constitution for India, the author declared that every citizen, i.e., anyone born in India, had a right to take part in the affairs of the country and be admitted to public office.
- The Motilal Nehru Report (1928) reaffirms this conception of citizenship, reiterating that every person of either sex who has attained the age of twenty-one is entitled to vote for the House of Representatives or Parliament.

FEDERALISM

- Constitution has created a strong central government.
- Unlike the constitutional symmetry of American federalism, Indian federalism has been constitutionally asymmetric.
- To meet the specific needs and requirements of some sub-units, it was always part of the original design to have a unique relationship with them or to give them special status.

- Under Article 371A, the privilege of special status was also accorded to the North-Eastern State of Nagaland.
- This Article not only confers validity on pre-existing laws within Nagaland, but also protects local identity through restrictions on immigration.
- Many other States too, are beneficiaries of such special provisions.
- According to the Indian Constitution, then, there is nothing bad about this differential treatment.
- Although the Constitution did not originally envisage this
- India is now a multi-lingual federation.
- Each major linguistic group is politically recognised and all are treated as equals.
- Thus, the democratic and linguistic federalism of India has managed to combine claims to unity with claims to cultural recognition.
- A fairly robust political arena exists that allows for the play of multiple identities that complement one another.

NATIONAL IDENTITY

- Constitution constantly reinforces a common national identity.
- India strives to retain regional identities along with the national identity.
- Common national identity was not incompatible with distinct religious or linguistic identities.
- The Indian Constitution tried to balance these various identities.
- Yet, preference was given to common identity under certain conditions.
- This is clarified in the debate over separate electorates based on religious identity which the Constitution rejects.
- Rather than forced unity, our Constitution sought to evolve true fraternity
- A goal dear to the heart of Dr. Ambedkar. As Sardar Patel put it, the main objective was to evolve 'one community'.

PROCEDURAL ACHIEVEMENTS

- Indian Constitution reflects a faith in political deliberation.
- Debates in the Assembly show that the makers of the Constitution wanted to be as inclusive in their approach as possible.
- Willingness of people to modify their existing preferences
- To justify outcomes by reference not to self-interest but to reasons.
- It also shows a willingness to recognise creative value in difference and disagreement.
- It reflects a spirit of compromise and accommodation.
- An open process of free deliberation among equals, then the compromise arrived in this manner can hardly be objected to.

- Commitment to the idea that decisions on the most important issues must be arrived at consensually rather than by majority vote is equally morally commendable.

CRITICISM OF CONSTITUTION

1. It is unwieldy
2. It is unrepresentative
3. It is alien to our conditions.

It is unwieldy

- Based on the assumption that the entire constitution of a country must be found in one compact document.
- It is possible to find important constitutional statements and practices outside one compact document.
- In the case of India, many such details, practices and statements are included in one single document and this has made that document somewhat large in size.
- Many countries for instance, do not have provisions for election commission or the civil service commission in the document known as constitution.
- But in India, many such matters are attended to by the Constitutional document itself.

It is unrepresentative

- How Constituent Assembly was formed?
- No adult franchise
- Most members came from the advanced sections of the society.

Does this make our Constitution unrepresentative?

- members of the Constituent Assembly were chosen by a restricted franchise, not by universal suffrage.
- almost every shade of opinion was represented in the Constituent Assembly
- a vast range of issues and opinions were discussed and debated

It is alien to our conditions

- borrowed article by article from western constitutions and sits uneasily with the cultural ethos of the Indian people.
- This criticism is often voiced by many.
- Even in the Constituent Assembly itself, there were some voices that echo this concern.

How far is this charge true?

- It is true that the Indian Constitution is modern and partly western.
- It was never a blind borrowing. It was innovative borrowing.
- When we were drafting our Constitution, efforts were made to amalgamate western and traditional Indian values.
- It was a process of selective adaptation and not borrowing.

LIMITATIONS

- All this is not to say that the Constitution of India is a perfect and flawless document.
- Given the social conditions within which the Constitution was made, it was only natural that there may be many controversial matters, that there would be many areas that needed careful revision.
- There are many features of this Constitution that have emerged mainly due to the exigencies of the time.
- Nonetheless, we must admit that there are many limitations to this Constitution.

Let us briefly mention the limitations of the Constitution.

- First, the Indian Constitution has a centralised idea of national unity.
- Second, it appears to have glossed over some important issues of gender justice, particularly within the family.
- Third, it is not clear why in a poor developing country, certain basic socio-economic rights were relegated to the section on Directive Principles rather than made an integral feature of our fundamental rights.

16 Political Theory

STUDY OF POLITICAL THEORY

- The study of various principles, ideas and ideals that inspire people and guide government to frame public policies like freedom, equality etc.
- Basic ides of Political Theory – Institutions around us –Legislature/Judiciary/Executive based on basic ideas/values- we study about these ideas and theories in Political Theory
- Political Theory - Study of values and ideas that guide institutions around us

WHY IS POLITICAL THEORY STUDIED ?

- It gives us the basic knowledge about political principles, and ideas.
- It helps us in examining our understanding of be political system in the country.
- It helps in demarking just and unjust actions of the government.
- It is used by all eminent professionals.

OBJECTIVE OF POLITICAL THEORY

- The human beings have capabilities to act and react to different situations. They can converse with each other and reasonably discuss issues and settle disputes.
- Political Theory systematically thinks about the values that inform political life - values such as freedom, equality and justice.
- The objective of political theory is to train citizens to think rationally about political questions and assess the political events of our time.
- Politics is an important and integral part of any society.
- Politics, at one level, involves what governments do and how they relate to the aspirations of the people, at another level, it involves how people struggle and influence decision making.

POLITICAL THEORY ANALYSES THE BASIC QUESTIONS SUCH AS

- How a country must be organised?
- why do we need a government ?
- what do we owe to each other as citizens.?

WHAT IS POLITICAL THEORY?

- Political theory is concerned with the ideas and principles that systematically shape the constitution, governments, and social life.
- Certain values and principles, such as democracy, freedom, and equality, have inspired people and guided policies.
- The origins of these values and words need to be understood rationally and political theory helps us in that respect.
- Political theory explains what freedom, equality, justice, democracy, secularism, and other concepts mean.

RELEVANCE OF POLITICAL THEORIES IN INDIA

- In the Indian Constitution, our Preamble enshrines freedom and equality; the chapter on Rights in the Indian Constitution abolishes Untouchability in any form; Gandhian principles find a place in Directive Principles.
- Political theory deals with the ideas and the principles that shape Constitutions, governments and social life in a systematic manner.
- The Fundamental rights guaranteed by our Constitution are continually being reinterpreted in response to new circumstances.
- The Right to Life has been interpreted by the Courts to include the Right to Livelihood.
- As our world changes, we may discover new dimensions of freedom as well as new threats to freedom.
- For instance, global communications technology is making it easier for activists to network with one another across the world for protecting tribal cultures of forests. But, it also enables terrorists and criminals to network.

PUTTING POLITICAL THEORY TO PRACTICE

- Political theorists clarify the meaning of political concepts by looking at how they are understood and used in ordinary language.
- They also debate and examine the diverse meanings and opinions in a systematic manner.
- A Political theory is relevant for all the groups to act responsibly as a citizen, it is helpful to have a basic knowledge of the political ideas and institutions that shape the world we live in.
- It is crucial that we learn to be reasonable and informed if we are to participate in Gram Sabhas or offer our views on websites and polls.
- An educated and vigilant citizenry makes those, who play politics, more public-spirited.
- As students, we have opinions about what is right or wrong, just or unjust, but do not know whether they are reasonable or not.
- Political Theory exposes us to systematic thinking on justice or equality so that we can polish our opinions and argue in an informed manner and for the sake of common interests.

What is Freedom

- The term 'Swaraj' incorporates within it two words-Swa (Self) and Raj (Rule).
- It can be understood to mean both the rule of the self and rule over self.
- A simple answer to the question 'what is freedom' is absence of constraints.

- Freedom is also about expanding the ability of people to freely express themselves and develop their potential.

- To be free, a society must widen the area in which individuals, groups, communities or nations, will be able to charter their own destiny and be what they wish to be.

- Freedom allows the full development of the individual's creativity, sensibilities and capabilities.

- Both these aspects of freedom — the absence of external constraints as well as the existence of conditions in which people can develop their talents — are important.

- A free society would be one which enables all its members to develop their potential with the minimum of social constraints.

- No individual living in society can hope to enjoy total absence of any kind of constraints or restrictions.

- It becomes necessary then to determine which social constraints are justified and which are not, which are acceptable and which should be removed.

- To understand which social constraints are necessary, discussions on freedom need to look at the core relationship between the individual and the society (or group, community, or state) within which she/he is placed.

- That is, we need to examine the relationship between individual and society

CONSTRAINTS OF FREEDOM

- Restrictions on the freedom of individuals may come from domination and external controls.

- Such restrictions may be imposed by force or they may be imposed by a government through laws

- apartheid in South Africa.

- democratic government is considered to be an important means of protecting the freedom of people.

- Constraints on freedom can also result from social inequality of the kind implicit in the caste system, or which result from extreme economic inequality in a society.

- The quotation from Subhas Chandra Bose on freedom draws attention to the need for the country to work to remove such constraints.

Why do we need constraints?

- We cannot live in a world where there are no constraints.

- We need some political and legal restraints to ensure that differences may be discussed and debated without one group coercively imposing its view on the other.

- Liberalism acknowledges a role for welfare state and accepts the need for measures to reduce both social and economic inequalities.

- It is the state which can constrain a person from acting in a way that causes harm to someone else.

- Constraining actions by the force of law should only happen when the other restraining actions cause serious harm to definite individuals.

- Ideally, in a free society we should be able to hold our views, develop our own rules of living, and pursue our choices.

- But the creation of such a society too requires some constraints.
- At the very least, it requires that we be willing to respect differences of views, opinions and beliefs.
- Sometimes strong commitment to our beliefs requires that we must oppose all those who differ from or reject our views.
- We see their views or ways of living as unacceptable or even undesirable.
- Under such circumstances we need some legal and political restraints to ensure that differences may be discussed and debated without one group coercively imposing its views on the other.

FREEDOM OF EXPRESSION

- Freedom of expression is a fundamental value and for that society must be willing to bear some inconvenience to protect it from people who want to restrict it.
- At various times there have been demands to ban books, plays, films, or academic articles in research journals.
- Justifiable constraints' supported by proper procedures and important moral arguments.
- Voltaire stated - "I disapprove of what you say but I will defend to death your right to say it."
- Banning is an easy solution for the short term since it meets the immediate demand but is very harmful for the long-term prospects of freedom in a society because once one begins to ban, then one develops a habit of banning.
- If we are not coerced into accepting the conditions, then we cannot claim that our freedom has been curtailed.
- We began by saying that freedom is the absence of external constraints. We have now come to realise that freedom embodies our capacity and our ability to make choices. And when we make choices, we have also to accept responsibility for our actions and their consequences. It is for this reason that most advocates of liberty and freedom maintain that children must be placed in the care of parents. Our capacity to make the right choices, to assess in a reasoned manner available options, and shoulder the responsibility of our actions, have to be built through education and cultivation of judgement just as much as it needs to be nurtured by limiting the authority of the state and the society.

Equality

CONCEPT OF EQUALITY

- The concept of equality implies that all people, as human beings, are entitled to the same rights and opportunities to develop their skills and talents, and to pursue their goals and ambitions.
- It is not the lack of equality of status or wealth or privilege that is significant but the inequalities in people's access to such basic goods, as education, health care, safe housing, that make for an unequal and unjust society.
- It is difficult to use the natural / socially-produced distinction as a standard by which the laws and policies of a society can be assessed.

THE THREE DIMENSIONS OF EQUALITY

- **Political Equality** - It includes granting equal citizenship to all members of the state like freedom of expression, movement, association and belief. It includes legal rights guaranteed by the Constitution and the laws. A demand is often made for equal opportunities.
- **Social Equality** - It guarantees certain minimum conditions of life to all the members of the society - adequate health care, the opportunity for good education, adequate nourishment and a minimum wage. The state should make policies to prevent discrimination or harassment of women in public places or employment, to provide incentives to open up education or certain professions to women.
- **Economic Equality** - It exists in a society if there are significant differences in wealth, property or income between individuals or classes.

HOW CAN WE PROMOTE EQUALITY?

- The first step towards bringing about equality is ending the formal system of inequality and privileges.
- The Constitution of India prohibits discrimination on grounds of religion, race, caste, sex, or place of birth and abolishes the practice of Untouchability.
- Sometimes, it is necessary to treat people differently in order to ensure that they can enjoy equal rights.

- Disabled people may justifiably demand special ramps in public spaces.
- These should not be seen as infringements of equality but as enhancement of equality.

Affirmative Action

- Affirmative Action is based on the idea that it is not sufficient to establish formal equality by law.
- It is necessary to take some more positive measures to minimize and eliminate entrenched forms of social inequalities. Example for this can be policy of quotas or reserved seats in education and jobs.
- Critics of positive discrimination contend that any provision of reservations or quotas for the deprived in admissions for higher education or jobs is unfair as it arbitrarily denies other sections of society their right to equal treatment.
- Reservations are a form of reverse discrimination.
- A distinction is made between treating everyone in an identical manner and treating everyone as equal.
- Women require special facilities in order to exercise right to work. They require some provision for maternity leave and crèches in the workplace.

Reverse discrimination

- It is a term for discrimination against members of a dominant or majority group, in favour of members of a minority or historically disadvantaged group.
- Groups may be defined in terms of ethnicity, gender identity, nationality, race, religion, sex, or sexual orientation.

18   Social Justice

WHAT IS JUSTICE ?

- All cultures and traditions have grappled with questions of justice although they may have interpreted the concept in different ways. For instance, in ancient Indian society, justice was associated with dharma and maintaining dharma or a just social order, was considered to be a primary duty of kings. In China, Confucius, the famous philosopher argued that kings should maintain justice by punishing wrong doers and rewarding the virtuous.

- In fourth century B.C. Athens (Greece), Plato discussed issues of justice in his book The Republic.

- The idea that justice involves giving each person his due continues to be an important part of our present day understanding of justice. However, our understanding of what is due to a person has changed from the time of Plato. Today, our understanding of what is just is closely linked to our understanding of what is due to each person as a human being. According to the German philosopher Immanuel Kant, human beings possess dignity. If all persons are granted dignity then what is due to each of them is that they have the opportunity to develop their talents and pursue their chosen goals. Justice requires that we give due and equal consideration to all individuals

PRINCIPLES OF JUSTICE

- The principle of treating the equals equally requires that people should not be discriminated against on grounds of class, caste, race or gender. They should be judged on the basis of their work and actions and not on the basis of the group to which they belong.

- Although people should get the same reward for the same work, it would be fair and just to reward different kinds of work differently if we take into account factors such as the effort required, the skills required, the possible dangers involved in that work etc.

- The third principle of justice is for a society to take into account special needs of people while distributing rewards or duties.

- The principle of taking account of the special needs of people does not necessarily contradict the principle of equal treatment so much as extend it because the principle of treating equals equally could imply that people who are not equal in certain important respects could be treated differently.

Promote Just Society

- It becomes a function of governments to harmonise the different principles to promote a just society.

- Within a country, social justice would require not only that people be treated equally in terms of the laws and policies of the society but also that they enjoy some basic equality of life conditions and opportunities.

- John Rawls argues that the only way we can arrive at a fair and just rule is if we imagine ourselves to be in a situation in which we have to make decisions about how society should be organised although we do not know which position we would ourselves occupy in that society.

- He describes this as thinking under a 'veil of ignorance'. He expects that in such a situation, each will envisage the future society from the point of view of the worst-off.

Veil of ignorance

- John Rawls argues that the only way we can arrive at a fair and just rule is if we imagine ourselves to be in a situation in which we have to make decisions about how society should be organised although we do not know which position we would ourselves occupy in that society.

- He describes this as thinking under a 'veil of ignorance'.

- Rawls suggests that you imagine yourself in an original position behind a veil of ignorance. Behind this veil, you know nothing of yourself and your natural abilities, or your position in society. Behind such a veil of ignorance all individuals are simply specified as rational, free, and morally equal beings.

- The merit of the 'veil of ignorance' position is that it expects people to just be their usual rational themselves, they are expected to think for themselves and choose what they regard to be in their interest - when they choose under the 'veil of ignorance' they will find that it is in their interest to think from the position of the worst-off.

- Rawls argues that rational thinking, not morality, could lead us to be fair and judge impartially regarding how to distribute the benefits and burdens of a society.

- A just society should provide people with the basic minimum conditions to enable them to live healthy and secure lives and develop their talents as well as equal opportunities to pursue their chosen goals in society.

Justice as Fairness

- The basic amount of nourishment needed to remain healthy, housing, supply of clean drinking water, education and a minimum wage constitute an important part of the basic minimum conditions of life needed by the people.

- Supporters of the free market believe that if markets are left free of state interference, the sum of market transactions would ensure overall a just distribution of benefits and duties in society.

- Those with merit and talent would be awarded accordingly while the incompetent would get a lesser reward.

PURSUING SOCIAL JUSTICE

- States could step in to ensure a basic minimum standard of living to all people so that they are able to compete on equal terms.

- The most efficient way of providing people with basic services might be to allow the development of markets in healthcare, education and similar other services.

- Private agencies should be encouraged to provide such services while state policies should try to empower people to buy those services.

- Free markets often exhibit a tendency to work in favour of the already privileged.

- To ensure social justice, the state should step in to see that basic facilities are made available to all the members of a society.

- In our own country, many kinds of social and economic inequalities exist and much remains to be done if they are to be reduced.

19

Rights

WHAT ARE RIGHTS?

- In everyday life we often talk of our rights.
- As members of a democratic country we may speak of such rights as the right to vote, the right to form political parties, the right to contest elections and so on.
- But apart from the generally accepted political and civil rights, people today are also making new demands for rights such as the right to information, right to clean air or the right to safe drinking water.
- A right is essentially an entitlement or a justified claim.
- It denotes what we are entitled to as citizens, as individuals and as human beings.
- It is something that we consider to be due to us; something that the rest of society must recognize as being a legitimate claim that must be upheld
- Rights are legal, social, or ethical principles of freedom or entitlement; that is, rights are the fundamental normative rules about what is allowed of people or owed to people according to some legal system, social convention, or ethical theory. Rights are primarily those claims that are necessary for leading a life of respect and dignity. It is something that is considered to be due to an individual; something that the rest of society must recognize as being a legitimate claim that must be upheld.

THE HISTORY OF RIGHTS

- Political theorists in the seventeenth and eighteenth centuries argued that God's nature bestows rights on us.
- They claimed to have derived them from natural law.
- This meant that rights are not bestowed by a ruler or society; rather, they are bestowed upon us at birth.

There are three natural rights identified by the early political theorists:

- Right to Life
- Right to liberty

- Right to property.

All the other rights were said to be derived from these basic rights.

WHERE DO RIGHTS COME FROM?

- In the seventeenth and eighteenth centuries, political theorists argued that rights are given to us by nature or God.
- The rights of men were derived from natural law.
- This meant that rights were not conferred by a ruler or a society, rather we are born with them.
- The idea that we are born with certain rights, is a very powerful notion because it implies that no state or organisation should take away what has been given by the law of nature.
- This conception of natural rights has been used widely to oppose the exercise of arbitrary power by states and governments and to safeguard individual freedom.
- In recent years, the term human rights is being used more than the term natural rights.
- This is because the idea of there being a natural law, or a set of norms that are laid down for us by nature, or God, appears unacceptable today.
- Rights are increasingly seen as guarantees that human beings themselves seek or arrive at in order to lead a minimally good life.
- As a human being each person is unique and equally valuable.
- This means that all persons are equal and no one is born to serve others.
- Each of us possesses an intrinsic value, hence we must have equal opportunities to be free and realise our full potential.
- This conception of a free and equal self is increasingly being used to challenge existing inequalities based on race, caste, religion and gender.
- Today, the UN Universal Declaration of Human Rights builds upon this understanding of rights and it attempts to recognise those claims that the world community collectively sees as being important for leading a life of dignity and self-respect.
- The notion of universal human rights has been used by oppressed people all over the world to challenge laws which segregate them and deny them equal opportunities and rights.
- In fact, it is through the struggles of groups that have felt excluded that the interpretation of existing rights has sometimes been altered.
- Slavery has, for instance, been abolished, but there are other struggles that have only had a limited success.
- Even today there are communities struggling to define humanity in a way which includes them
- The list of human rights which people have claimed has expanded over the years as societies face new threats and challenges.
- For instance, we are very conscious today of the need to protect the natural environment and this has generated demands for rights to clean air, water, sustainable development, and the like.

KINDS OF RIGHTS

- Most democracies today begin by drawing up a charter of political rights.
- Political rights give to the citizens the right to equality before law and the right to participate in the political process.

They include such rights as the

- ▶ right to vote and elect representatives
- ▶ the right to contest elections
- ▶ the right to form political parties or join them
- Political rights are supplemented by civil liberties.
- The latter refers to the right to a free and fair trial, the right to express one's views freely, the right to protest and express dissent.
- Collectively, civil liberties and political rights form the basis of a democratic system of government. But, as was mentioned before, rights aim to protect the well-being of the individual.
- Political rights contribute to it by making the government accountable to the people, by giving greater importance to the concerns of the individual over that of the rulers and by ensuring that all persons have an opportunity to influence the decisions of the government.
- However, our rights of political participation can only be exercised fully when our basic needs, of food, shelter, clothing, health, are met.
- For a person living on the pavements and struggling to meet these basic needs, political rights by themselves have little value.
- They require certain facilities like an adequate wage to meet their basic needs and reasonable conditions of work.
- Hence democratic societies are beginning to recognise these obligations and providing economic rights
- In some countries, citizens, particularly those with low incomes, receive housing and medical facilities from the state; in others, unemployed persons receive a certain minimum wage so that they can meet their basic needs.
- In India the government has recently introduced a rural employment guarantee scheme, among other measures to help the poor.
- Today, in addition to political and economic rights more and more democracies are recognising the cultural claims of their citizens
- The right to have primary education in one's mother tongue, the right to establish institutions for teaching one's language and culture, are today recognised as being necessary for leading a good life.
- The list of rights has thus steadily increased in democracies. While some rights, primarily the right to life, liberty, equal treatment, and the right to political participation are seen as basic rights that must receive priority, other conditions that are necessary for leading a decent life, are being recognised as justified claims or rights.

RIGHTS AND RESPONSIBILITIES

- Rights not only place obligations upon the state to act in a certain way — for instance, to ensure sustainable development — but they also place obligations upon each of us.

- Firstly, they compel us to think not just of our own personal needs and interests but to defend some things as being good for all of us. Protecting the ozone layer, minimising air and water pollution, maintaining the green cover by planting new trees and preventing cutting down of forests, maintaining the ecological balance, are things that are essential for all of us. They represent the 'common-good' that we must act to protect for ourselves as well as for the future generations who are entitled to inherit a safe and clean world without which they cannot lead a reasonably good life.

- Secondly, they require that I respect the rights of others. If I say that I must be given the right to express my views I must also grant the same right to others. If I do not want others to interfere in the choices I make — the dress I wear or the music I listen to — I must refrain from interfering in the choices that others make. I must leave them free to choose their music and clothes. I cannot use the right to free speech to incite a crowd to kill my neighbour. In exercising my rights, I cannot deprive others of their rights. My rights are, in other words, limited by the principle of equal and same rights for all.

- Thirdly, we must balance our rights when they come into conflict. For instance, my right to freedom of expression allows me to take pictures; however, if I take pictures of a person bathing in his house without his consent and post them on the internet, that would be a violation of his right to privacy.

- Fourthly, citizens must be vigilant about limitations which may be placed on their rights. A currently debated topic concerns the increased restrictions which many governments are imposing on the civil liberties of citizens on the grounds of national security. Protecting national security may be defended as necessary for safeguarding the rights and well-being of citizens. But at what point could the restrictions imposed as necessary for security themselves become a threat to the rights of people? In such situations the question to ask is whether the person concerned poses an imminent threat to society. Even arrested persons should be allowed legal counsel and the opportunity to present their case before a magistrate or a court of law.

20 Citizenship and Secularism

CITIZENSHIP

- Citizenship implies full and equal membership of a political community.
- In the contemporary world, states provide a collective political identity to their members as well as certain rights.
- Citizens expect certain rights from their state as well as help and protection wherever they may travel.
- The precise nature of the rights granted to citizens may vary from state to state but in most democratic countries today they would include some political rights like the right to vote, civil rights like the freedom of speech or belief, and some socio-economic rights which could include the right to a minimum wage, or the right to education. Equality of rights and status is one of the basic rights of citizenship.
- Earliest struggles were fought by people to assert their independence and rights against powerful monarchies.
- Many European countries experienced such struggles, some of them violent, like the French Revolution in 1789.
- In the colonies of Asia and Africa, demands for equal citizenship formed part of their struggle for independence from colonial rulers.
- In South Africa, the black African population had to undertake a long struggle against the ruling white minority for equal citizenship. This continued until the early 1990s.
- Struggles to achieve full membership and equal rights continue even now in many parts of the world. E.g. women's movement and dalit movement in our country.
- Citizenship is about more than the relationship between states and their members.
- It is also about citizen-citizen relations and involves certain obligations of citizens to each other and to the society.
- These would include not just the legal obligations imposed by states but also a moral obligation to participate in, and contribute to, the shared life of the community.
- Citizens are also considered to be the inheritors and trustees of the culture and natural resources of the country.

CITIZEN AND NATION

- The concept of nation state evolved in the modern period.
- Earliest assertions regarding sovereignty of nation state and democratic rights of citizens was made in France in 1789.
- Nation states claim that their boundaries define not just a territory but also a unique culture and shared history.
- The national identity may be expressed through symbols like a flag, national anthem, national language, or certain ceremonial practices, among other things.
- Most modern states include people of different religions, languages, and cultural traditions.
- But the national identity of a democratic state is supposed to provide citizens with a political identity that can be shared by all the members of the state.
- Democratic states usually try to define their identity so that it is as inclusive as possible — that is, which allows all citizens to identify themselves as part of the nation. (rt to vote, acquire property)
- But in practice, most countries tend to define their identity in a way which makes it easier for some citizens to identify with the state than others.(citizen v/s NRI)
- It may also make it easier for the state to extend citizenship to some people and not others. (adnan sami)
- This would be as true of the United States, which prides itself on being a country of immigrants, as any other country.
- France is a country which claims to be both secular and inclusive.
- It includes not only people of European origin but also citizens who originally came from other areas such as North Africa.
- Culture and language are important features of its national identity and all citizens are expected to assimilate into it in the public aspects of their lives.
- They may, however, retain their personal beliefs and practices in their private lives.
- Religious belief is supposed to belong to the private sphere of citizens but sometimes religious symbols and practices may enter into their public lives. Ex- Sikh school boys in France to wear the turban to school, and of Muslim girls to wear the head scarf with their school uniforms

GRANTING CITIZENSHIP

- The criteria for granting citizenship to new applicants varies from country to country. In countries such as Israel, or Germany, factors like religion, or ethnic origin, may be given priority when granting citizenship.
- In Germany there has been a persistent demand from Turkish workers, who were at one time encouraged to come and work in Germany, that their children who have been born and brought up in Germany should automatically be granted citizenship.
- India defines itself as a secular, democratic, nation state. The movement for independence was a broad based one and deliberate attempts were made to bind together people of different religions, regions and cultures.

- True, Partition of the country did take place in 1947 when differences with the Muslim League could not be resolved, but this only strengthened the resolve of Indian national leaders to maintain the secular and inclusive character of the Indian nation state they were committed to build. This resolve was embodied in the Constitution.

- Indian Constitution - accommodate a very diverse society.

- It attempted to provide full and equal citizenship to groups like SC & ST, many women not previously enjoyed equal rights, remote communities in A&N islands who had had little contact with modern civilization, and many others.

- It also attempted to find a place for the different languages, religions and practices found in different parts of the country.

- The Republic Day parade in Delhi symbolises the attempt of the state to include people of different regions, cultures and religions.

- The provisions about citizenship in the Constitution can be found in Part Two and in subsequent laws passed by Parliament.

- The Constitution adopted an essentially democratic and inclusive notion of citizenship.

- In India, citizenship can be acquired by birth, descent, registration, naturalization, or inclusion of territory.

- The rights and obligations of citizens are listed in the Constitution.

- There is also a provision that the state should not discriminate against citizens on grounds only of religion, race, caste, sex, place of birth, or any of them.

- The rights of religious and linguistic minorities are also protected.

UNIVERSAL CITIZENSHIP

- When we think of refugees, or illegal migrants, many images may come to mind.

- e.g. people from Asia or Africa who have paid agents to smuggle them into Europe or America.

- e.g. people displaced by war or famine. Such images are often shown on the television.

- Refugees in the Darfur region of Sudan, Palestinians, Burmese or Bangladeshis, the examples are many.

- All these are people who have been forced to become refugees in their own, or neighboring countries.

- Many states may support the idea of universal and inclusive citizenship, each of them also fixes criteria for the grant of citizenship.

- These would generally be written into the Constitution and laws of the country.

- States use their power to keep unwanted visitors out.

- If no state is willing to accept them and they cannot return home, they become stateless peoples or refugees. They may be forced to live in camps, or as illegal migrants. Often they cannot legally work, or educate their children, or acquire property. The problem is so great that the U.N. has appointed a High Commissioner for Refugees to try to help them.

- Decisions regarding how many people can be absorbed as citizens in a country poses a difficult humanitarian and political problem for many states.
- Many countries have a policy of accepting those fleeing from persecution or war.
- But they may not want to accept unmanageable number of people or expose the country to security risks.
- India prides itself on providing refuge to persecuted peoples, as it did with the Dalai Lama and his followers in 1959.
- Entry of people from neighbouring countries has taken place along all the borders of the Indian state and the process continues.
- Many of these people remain as stateless peoples for many years or generations, living in camps, or as illegal migrants.
- Only a relatively few of them are eventually granted citizenship.
- Although many people cannot achieve citizenship of a state of their choice, no alternative identity exists for them.

GLOBAL CITIZENSHIP

- Supporters of global citizenship argue that although a world community and global society does not yet exist, people already feel linked to each other across national boundaries.
- E.g. outpouring of help from all parts of the world for victims of the Asian tsunami and other major calamities is a sign of the emergence of a global society.
- The concept of national citizenship assumes that our state can provide us with the protection and rights which we need to live with dignity in the world today.
- But states today are faced with many problems which they cannot tackle by themselves.
- One notion of global citizenship is that it might make it easier to deal with problems which extend across national boundaries and which therefore need cooperative action by the people and governments of many states.
- For instance, it might make it easier to find an acceptable solution to the issue of migrants and stateless peoples, or at least to ensure them basic rights and protection regardless of the country in which they may be living.
- The concept of global citizenship reminds us that national citizenship might need to be supplemented by an awareness that we live in an interconnected world and that there is also a need for us to strengthen our links with people in different parts of the world and be ready to work with people and governments across national boundaries.

NATIONALISM

- Nationalism has emerged as one of the most compelling of political creeds which has helped to shape history.
- It has inspired intense loyalties as well as deep hatreds.
- It has united people as well as divided them, helped to liberate them from oppressive rule as well as been the cause of conflict and bitterness and wars.

- It has been a factor in the break up of empires and states.
- Nationalist struggles have contributed to the drawing and redrawing of the boundaries of states and empires.
- At present a large part of the world is divided into different nation-states although the process of re-ordering of state boundaries has not come to an end and separatist struggles within existing states are common.
- Nationalism has passed through many phases.
- 19th century Europe, it led to the unification of a number of small kingdoms into larger nation-states.
- The present-day German and Italian states were formed through such a process of unification and consolidation.
- A large number of new states were also founded in Latin America.
- Along with the consolidation of state boundaries, local dialects and local loyalties were also gradually consolidated into state loyalties and common languages.
- The people of the new states acquired a new political identity which was based on membership of the nation-state.
- But nationalism also accompanied and contributed to the break up of large empires such as the Austro-Hungarian and Russian empires in the early twentieth century in Europe as well as the break-up of the British, French, Dutch and Portuguese empires in Asia and Africa.
- The struggle for freedom from colonial rule by India and other former colonies were nationalist struggles, inspired by the desire to establish nation-states which would be independent of. foreign control . The process of redrawing state boundaries continues to take place.
- Since 1960, even apparently stable nation-states have been confronted by nationalist demands put forward by groups or regions and these may include demands for separate statehood.
- Today, in many parts of the world we witness nationalist struggles that threaten to divide existing states.
- Such separatist movements have developed among the Quebecois in Canada, the Basques in northern Spain, the Kurds in Turkey and Iraq, and the Tamils in Sri Lanka, among others.
- The language of nationalism is also used by some groups in India.

Nations and Nationalism

- A nation is to a great extent an 'imagined' community, held together by the collective beliefs, aspirations and imaginations of its members.
- It is based on certain assumptions which people make about the collective whole with which they identify.
- Nation- An 'imagined' community, held together by the collective beliefs, aspirations and imaginations of its members

- Nationalism - The right of self-determination to imply that every nation in the world should exercise a right to determine its destiny in all walks of life w without interference of other states in the world members.
- State - A group of people having sovereignty, living in a fixed territory under the control of an organized government.

Shared Beliefs

- First, a nation is constituted by belief.
- It is refer to the collective identity and vision for the future of a group which aspires to have an independent political existence.
- A nation exists when its members believe that they belong together.

History

- Second, people who see themselves as a nation also embody a sense of continuing historical identity.
- They articulate for themselves a sense of their own history by drawing on collective memories, legends, historical records, to outline the continuing identity of the nation.
- Thus nationalists in India invoked its ancient civilisation and cultural heritage and other achievements to claim that India has had a long and continuing history as a civilisation and that this civilizational continuity and unity is the basis of the Indian nation.
- Jawaharlal Nehru wrote in his book The Discovery of India, "Though outwardly there was diversity and infinite variety among the people, everywhere there was that tremendous impress of oneness, which held all of us together in ages past, whatever political fate or misfortune had befallen us".

Territory

- Third, nations identify with a particular territory.
- Sharing a common past and living together on a particular territory over a long period of time gives people a sense of their collective identity.
- It helps them to imagine themselves as one people.
- Nations characterize the homeland in different ways, for instance as motherland, or fatherland, or holy land.
- The Jewish people for instance, in spite of being dispersed and scattered in different parts of the world always claimed that their original homeland was in Palestine, the 'promised land'.
- The Indian nation identifies with the rivers, mountains and regions of the Indian subcontinent.
- However, since more than one set of people may lay claim to the same territory, the aspiration for a homeland has been a major cause of conflict in the world.

Shared Political Ideals

- Fourth, it is a shared vision of the future and the collective aspiration to have an independent political existence that distinguishes groups from nations.
- Members of a nation share a vision of the kind of state they want to build.

- They affirm among other things a set of values and principles such as democracy, secularism and liberalism.
- These ideals represent the terms under which they come together and are willing to live together.
- It represents their political identity as a nation.
- In a democracy, it is shared commitment to a set of political values and ideals that is the most desirable basis of a political community or a nation-state.
- Within it, members of political community are bound by a set of obligations.
- These obligations arise from the recognition of the rights of each other as citizens.
- A nation is strengthened when its people acknowledge and accept their obligations to their fellow members.
- Recognition of this framework of obligations is the strongest test of loyalty to the nation.

Common Political Identity

- Many people believe that a shared political vision about the state and society we wish to create is not enough to bind individuals together as a nation.
- They seek instead a shared cultural identity, such as a common language, or common descent.
- Sharing the same religion gives us a set of common beliefs and social practices.
- But it can also pose a threat to the values that we cherish in a democracy.
- Democracies need to emphasise and expect loyalty to a set of values that may be enshrined in the Constitution of the country rather than adherence to a particular religion, race or language.

NATIONAL SELF DETERMINATION

- Nations seek the right to govern themselves and determine their future development.
- They seek the right to self-determination.
- In making this claim a nation seeks recognition and acceptance by the international community of its status as a distinct political entity or state.
- In some cases such claims are linked to the desire to form a state in which the culture of the group is protected if not privileged.
- Claims of the notion of one culture - one state began to gain acceptability in nineteenth century in Europe.
- The idea of one culture - one state was employed while reordering state boundaries after World War I.
- The Treaty of Versailles established a number of small, newly independent states, but it proved virtually impossible to satisfy all the demands for self-determination which were made at the time.
- Besides, re-organisation of state boundaries to satisfy the demands of one culture - one state, led to mass migration of population across state boundaries.

- Millions of people as a consequence were displaced from their homes and expelled from the land which had been their home for generations.
- Many others became victims of communal violence.
- Humanity paid a heavy price for re-organising boundaries in a way that culturally distinct communities could form separate nation-states.
- Besides, even in this effort it was not possible to ensure that the newly created states contained only one ethnic community.
- Indeed, most states had more than one ethnic and cultural community living within its boundaries.
- These communities, which were often small in number and constituted a minority within the state were often disadvantaged.
- Hence, the problem of accommodating minorities as equal citizens remained.
- The only positive aspect of these developments was that it granted political recognition to various groups who saw themselves as distinct nations and wanted the opportunity to govern themselves and determined their own future.
- The right to national self-determination has also been asserted by national liberation movements in Asia and Africa when they were struggling against colonial domination.
- Nationalist movements maintained that political independence would provide dignity and recognition to the colonised people and also help them to protect the collective interests of their people.
- Most national liberation movements were inspired by the goal of bringing justice and rights and prosperity to the nation.
- Migration of populations, border wars, and violence have continued to plague many countries in the region.
- Paradoxical situation, nation-states which themselves had achieved independence through struggle now acting against minorities within their own territories who claim the right to national self- determination.
- The solution does not lie in creating new states but in making existing states more democratic and equal.
- In ensuring that people with different cultural and ethnic identities live and co-exist as partners and equal citizens within the country.
- This may be essential not only for resolving problems arising from new claims for self-determination but also for building a strong and united states.

NATIONALISM AND PLURALISM

- The Indian constitution has an elaborate set of provisions for the protection of religious, linguistic and cultural minorities.
- The rights which have been granted in different countries include constitutional protection for the language, cultures, and religion, of minority groups and their members.

- In some cases, identified communities also have the right to representation as a group in legislative bodies and other state institutions.
- Such rights may be justified on the grounds that they provide equal treatment and protection of the law for members of these groups as well as protection for the cultural identity of the group.
- Different groups need to be granted recognition as a part of the national community.
- The national identity has to be defined in an inclusive manner which can recognize the importance and unique contribution of all the cultural communities within the state.
- Some groups may continue to demand separate statehood.
- Paradoxical when globalisation is also spreading in the world, but nationalist aspirations continue to motivate many groups and communities.
- The right to national self-determination was often understood to include the right to independent statehood for nationalities.
- It might lead to the formation of a number of states too small to be economically and politically viable and it could multiply the problems of minorities.
- The right has now been reinterpreted to mean granting certain democratic rights for a nationality within a state.
- The world we live in is one that is deeply conscious of the importance of giving recognition to identities.
- Today we witness many struggles for the recognition of group identities, many of which employ the language of nationalism.
- While we need to acknowledge the claims of identity, we should be careful not to allow identity claims to lead to divisions and violence in the society.
- We need to remember that each person has many identities.
- In a democracy the political identity of citizen should encompass the different identities which people may have.
- It would be dangerous if intolerant and homogenizing forms of identity and nationalism are allowed to develop.

SECULARISM

Two Kinds

1. **Western Notion**
2. **Indian Notion**

INDIAN SECULARISM

- Originally, India was not declared a secular state, the word secular was added by the 42nd Amendment Act.
- India used to believe since ancient times the nation of Sarva Dharm Sam Bhava (सर्व धर्म सम भाव) because India respects all religions equally.

What is Secularism ?

- The Constitution declares that every Indian citizen has a right to live with freedom and dignity in any part of the country.
- Secularism is first and foremost a doctrine that opposes all such forms of inter-religious domination.

Secularism is not anti-religious

- When religion is organised, it is taken over by its most conservative faction, which does not tolerate any dissent.
- Many religions fragment into sects which leads to frequent sectarian violence and persecution of dissenting minorities
- As secularism is opposed to all forms of institutionalised religious domination, it challenges not merely inter- religious as well as intra-religious domination.
- Intra-religious domination is the circumstances where a society or religion commands their own members belonging to a similar group.
- Inter religious domination can be described as agitation made by one dominant society or its members on other social groups on the event of their doctrinal identity

What is Secular State ?

- Secularism is a normative doctrine which seeks to realise a secular society, i.e., one devoid of either inter-religious or intra-religious domination.
- It promotes freedom within religions, and equality between, as well as within religions
- A Education is one way of helping to change the mind set of people.

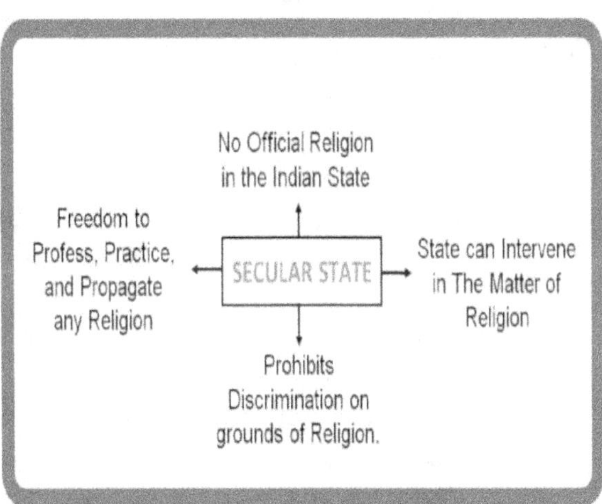

- A state must not be run by the heads of any particular religion.
- A state governed directly by a priestly order is called theocratic.
- To be truly secular, a state must not only refuse to be theocratic but also have no formal, legal alliance with any religion.

- A secular state must be committed to principles and goals which are partly derived from non-religious sources.
- Religious institutions and state institutions must be kept separate if we value peace, freedom, and equality.
- There are also states that are not theocratic but have a close relationship with a particular religion.
- Example: The state in England in the sixteenth century was not run by a priestly class but clearly favoured the Anglican Church and its members.
- England had an established Anglican religion, which was the official religion of the state.
- Today Pakistan has an official state religion, namely Sunni Islam. Such regimes may leave little scope for internal dissent or religious equality.

THEOCRATIC STATES

- A theocratic state is one that is governed directly by a priestly order.
- Theocratic states, such as the Papal States of Europe in mediaeval times or the Taliban-controlled state today, lack separation between religious and political institutions and are known for their hierarchies, oppressions, and unwillingness to allow members of other religious groups to practise their religion freely.

THE WESTERN MODEL OF SECULARISM

Mutual exclusion

- The state will not intervene in the affairs of religion and, in the same manner, religion will not interfere in the affairs of the state.
- No policy of the state can have an exclusively religious rationale.
- The state can neither aid any religious institution nor can it hinder the activities of religious communities.
- Religion is a private matter, not a matter of state policy or law.
- This form of secularism has no place for the idea of state-supported religious reform.

The Indian Model Of Secularism

- Indian secularism is fundamentally different from Western secularism.
- Indian secularism took on a distinct form as a result of an interaction between what already existed in a society that had religious diversity and the ideas that came from the west.
- Indian secularism equally opposed the oppression of dalits and women within Hinduism, the discrimination against women within Indian Islam or Christianity, and the possible threats that a majority community might pose to the rights of the minority religious communities.
- Indian secularism deals not only with religious freedom of individuals but also with religious freedom of minority communities.

- Indian secularism has made room for and is compatible with the idea of state-supported religious reform, bans Untouchability, abolishing child marriage and lifting the taboo on inter-caste marriage.
- Indian State has adopted a very sophisticated policy in pursuit of religious equality.
- This allows it either to disengage with religion in American style, or engage with it if required.
- The Indian state may engage with religion negatively to oppose religious tyranny.
- The Indian Constitution grants all religious minorities the right to establish and maintain their own educational institutions which may receive assistance from the state.
- The secular state does not have to treat every aspect of every religion with equal respect.
- It allows equal disrespect for some aspects of organised religions.

Indian secularism can be criticized on the grounds of being

- anti-religions
- imported from western culture
- charge of minoritism
- interventionist based on vote bank politics
- and it is considered to be an impossible project.

Anti-religious

- It is argued that secularism is anti-religious.
- We have shown that secularism is against institutionalised religious domination.
- It has been argued by some that secularism threatens religious identity.
- Actually, secularism promotes religious freedom and equality.

Western import

- Secularism is linked to Christianity, that it is western and therefore unsuited to Indian conditions.
- In reality, a secular state may keep a principled distance from religion to promote peace communities and it may also intervene to protect the rights of specific communities.

Minoritism

- Indian secularism advocates minority rights.
- The actual position is that when it comes to fundamental interests, voting as a democratic procedure is inappropriate.
- The most fundamental interest of minorities must not be harmed and must be protected by constitutional law.
- Minority rights are justified as long as these rights protect their fundamental interests.
- Minority rights need not be nor should be viewed as special privileges.

Interventionist

- Secularism is coercive and that it interferes excessively with the religious freedom of communities.
- Actually, Indian secularism follows the concept of principled distance which also allows for non-interference.
- The state must act as a facilitator by supporting liberal and democratic voices within every religion.

Vote Bank Politics

- Secularism encourages the politics of vote banks.
- If secular politicians who sought the votes of minorities also manage to give them what they want, then this is a success of the secular project.
- There is nothing wrong with vote bank politics as such, but only with a form of vote bank politics that generates injustice.

Impossible Project

- Secularism cannot work because it tries to do too much.
- People with deep religious differences will never live together in peace.
- But, the history of Indian civilisation shows that this kind of living together is realisable

21 — Peace

PEACE

- Peace occupied a central place in the original teachings of almost all religions.
- Humanity has learnt to value peace after paying a huge price for its absence.
- Today, life is more insecure than ever before as people everywhere face a growing threat from terrorism.
- Peace is often defined as the absence of war. The definition is simple but misleading.

PEACE AND THE STATE

- Division of world into separate sovereign states is an impediment to the pursuit of peace.
- As each state sees itself as an independent and supreme entity, it tends to protect its own perceived self-interest.
- Pursuit of peace - we see ourselves as part of the larger humanity, states tend to make distinctions between people.
- To pursue the interest of their citizens they are willing to inflict injury upon others.
- In today's world each state has consolidated instruments of coercion and force.
- While the state was expected to use its force, its army or its police, to protect its citizens, in practice these forces could be deployed against its own members to suppress dissent. e.g. Myanmar.
- The long-term solution lies in making the state more accountable through meaningful democratization and reining it in via an effective system of civil liberties. E.g. South Africa
- The struggle for democracy and human rights is closely linked to the safeguarding of peace.

DIFFERENT APPROACHES TO THE PURSUIT OF PEACE

- The first approach accords centrality to states, respects their sovereignty, and treats competition among them as a fact of life.
- Main concern proper management of this competition, and with the containment of possible conflict through inter-state arrangements like 'balance of power'.

- Such a balance was there in 19th century when the major European countries fine-tuned their struggle for power by forming alliances that deterred potential aggressors and prevented the outbreak of a large-scale war.
- The second approach too grants the deep-rooted nature of inter-state rivalry.
- But it stresses the positive presence and possibilities of interdependence.
- It underscores the growing social and economic cooperation among nations.
- Such cooperation is expected to temper state sovereignty and promote international understanding.
- Consequently global conflict would be reduced, leading to better prospects of peace.
- e.g. post-World War II Europe secured durable peace by graduating from economic integration to political unification.
- Third considers the state system to be a passing phase of human history.
- It envisages the emergence of a supra-national order and sees the fostering of a global community as the surest guarantee of peace.
- It can be done by expanding interactions and coalitions across state boundaries that involve diverse non-governmental actors like multinational corporations and people's movements.
- Proponents - ongoing process of globalization is further eroding the already diminished primacy and sovereignty of the state, thereby creating conditions conducive to the establishment of world peace.
- The United Nations may be said to embody elements of all the three approaches.
- The Security Council, which gives permanent membership and veto power (the right to shoot down a proposal even if it is supported by other members) to five dominant states, reflects the prevalent international hierarchy.
- The Economic and Social Council promotes inter-state cooperation in several spheres.
- The Commission on Human Rights seeks to shape and apply transnational norms

CONTEMPORARY CHALLENGES

- U.N.O. has several noteworthy achievements, it has not succeeded in preventing and eliminating threats to peace.
- Dominant states have asserted their sovereignty and sought to shape regional power structures and the international system itself in keeping with their own perceptions and priorities.
- To this end, they have even resorted to direct military action against and occupation of foreign territories. E.g. US intervention in Afghanistan and Iraq.
- The rise of terrorism is partly a response to the self-serving and ham-handed conduct of the aggressive states.
- Terrorists currently pose a great threat to peace through an adroit and ruthless use of modern weapons and advanced technology more generally. E.g. demolition of World Trade Centre (New York, USA) by Islamic militants on 11 September 2001.

- The use of biological/chemical/nuclear weapons of mass destruction by these forces remains a frightening possibility.
- The global community has failed to curb the rapacity of the domineering powers and the guerrilla tactics of the terrorists.
- e.g. genocide in Rwanda — an African country witnessed the murder of nearly half a million Tutsis by Hutus during 1994.
- After World War II, countries like Japan and Costa Rica decided not to maintain military forces.
- Several parts of the world, creation of nuclear -weapon-free zones where the use, development or deployment of nuclear weapons is banned through an internationally recognized treaty.
- Today there are six such zones covering the Antarctic territory, Latin America and the Caribbean, South-East Asia, Africa, the South Pacific, and Mongolia.
- The disintegration of the USSR in 1991 put a full stop to the era of military (especially nuclear) rivalry between the super powers.

22 Development

INTRODUCTION

- Development conveys the ideas of improvement, progress, well-being and an aspiration for a better life.

- Through its notion of development, a society articulates what constitutes its vision for the society as a whole and how best to achieve it.

- The term development is also often used in a narrower sense to refer to more limited goals such as increasing the rate of economic growth or modernising the society.

- Development has unfortunately often come to be identified with achieving pre-set targets, or completing projects like dams, or factories, hospitals, rather than with realising the broader vision of development which the society upholds.

- In the process some sections of society may have benefited while others may have had to suffer loss of their homes, or lands, or way of life, without any compensatory gains.

- Issues such as whether the rights of people have been respected in the course of development, whether the benefits and burdens of development have been justly distributed, or whether decisions regarding development priorities have been democratically made, have been raised in many countries.

- The models of development which have been adopted in different countries have become the subject of debate and criticism and alternative models have been put forward.

THE CHALLENGES OF DEVELOPMENT

- The concept of development gained importance after the second half of the twentieth century.

- This was the time when a large number of countries in Asia and Africa gained political independence.

- Most were impoverished and their populations had a low standard of living.

- Education, health and other facilities were poor.

- They were often described as 'underdeveloped' or 'developing'.

- The comparison was with the richer countries in Western Europe and the United States.
- In the 1950s and 1960s when most countries of Asia and Africa had achieved independence from colonial rule, the most urgent task in front of them was to solve the pressing problems of poverty, malnourishment, unemployment, illiteracy and the lack of basic amenities that a majority of their populations faced.
- They argued that the reason why they were backward was because under colonial rule their resources had been used not for their own benefit but for the benefit of their colonial masters.
- With Independence, they could reorganise their resources in the best possible manner to serve their national interests.
- Therefore it was now possible for them to formulate such policies which would allow them to overcome their backwardness and move towards achieving the standards of their former colonial masters.
- This provided the impetus for these countries to undertake development projects.
- In the initial years the focus was on catching up with the west in terms of economic growth and modernisation of societies.
- Developing countries adopted goals like faster economic growth through industrialisation, modernisation of agriculture and extending and modernising education.
- It was believed at the time that the state was the only agency capable of initiating this kind of social and economic change.
- Many countries embarked upon ambitious projects of development, often with the help of loans and aid from the developed countries.
- In India a series of Five Year Plans for development were made starting from the 1950s, and these included a number of mega projects such as the Bhakra Nangal Dam, setting up steel plants in different parts of the country, mining, fertilizer production and improving agricultural techniques.
- It was hoped that a multi-pronged strategy would have an impact on the economy and significantly increase the wealth of the country.
- It was also hoped that the emerging prosperity would gradually 'trickle down' to the poorest sections of society and help to reduce inequality.
- A great deal of faith was placed in adopting the latest discoveries of science and state of the art technologies.
- New educational institutions like the Indian Institutes of Technology were set up and collaboration with advanced countries in order to have access to their knowledge became a top priority.
- The model of development adopted by India and other countries has come under a great deal of criticism over the years and this has led to some rethinking about the goals and processes of development today.

CRITICISM OF DEVELOPMENT MODELS

- Critics of development have pointed out that the kind of development models which have been adopted in many countries has proved very costly for the developing countries.
- The financial costs have been enormous, putting many countries into long-term debt.
- Africa is still suffering from the enormous debts which it ran up by borrowings from the richer countries.
- The gains in terms of growth have not been commensurate and poverty and disease continue to plague the continent.

THE SOCIAL COST OF DEVELOPMENT

- This model of development has high social costs.
- A large number of people have been displaced from their homes and localities due to the construction of big dams, industrial activities and mining activities, or other projects.
- Displacement results in loss of livelihood and increases impoverishment.
- If rural agricultural communities are displaced from their traditional occupations and regions they end up at the margins of society, swelling the large number of urban and rural poor.
- Traditional skills acquired over an extended period may be lost.
- There is also a loss of culture because when people are relocated they lose a whole way of community life.
- Such displacement has led to struggles in many countries.
- Displaced people have not always accepted their fate passively. E.g. 'Narmada Bachao Andolan' has been leading a movement against the Sardar Sarovar Dam on the river Narmada for many years.

ENVIRONMENTAL COSTS OF DEVELOPMENT

- Development has indeed caused a high degree of environmental degradation in many countries.
- Global warming - ice in the Arctic and Antarctic is melting because of increased emission of greenhouse gases into the atmosphere and this has the potential to cause floods and actually submerge low lying areas like Bangladesh and the Maldives.
- In the long term, the ecological crisis will adversely affect all of us.
- Air pollution is already a problem which does not discriminate between the rich and the poor.
- But in the short term, indiscriminate use of resources tends to adversely affect the under-privileged more sharply.
- Loss of forests affects the poor who use forest resources for a variety of subsistence needs like firewood, medicinal herbs or food.
- Drying up of rivers and ponds and falling ground water levels means that women have to walk longer in order to procure water.
- The model of development we are pursuing is heavily dependent on the increasing use of energy.

- Most of the energy currently generated in the world is from non-renewable sources like coal or petroleum.
- Large tracts of the Amazon rainforests are being deforested in order to provide for the increased consumer needs.

ASSESSING DEVELOPMENT

- Some countries have had some success in increasing their rate of economic growth and even in reducing poverty.
- But overall, inequalities have not been seriously reduced and poverty continues to be a problem in the developing world.
- However, the world over, the gap between the rich and the poor has been widening.
- A country may have high rates of growth but that doesn't necessarily translate into a fair distribution of its benefits.
- When economic growth and redistribution do not go together, the benefits are likely to be cornered by those who are already privileged.
- It is now increasingly being recognised that there is a need to adopt a broader notion of development.
- An excessive focus on economic growth has not only given rise to a wide range of problems but even economic growth has not always been satisfactory.
- Hence, development is now being viewed in broader terms as a process which should improve the quality of life of all the people.
- If development is understood as a process which aims to improve the quality of life of people, it could be argued that measuring the rate of economic growth alone would be an inadequate and at times misleading indicator of development.
- Human Development Report which is annually brought out by the United Nations Development Programme (UNDP).
- This report ranks countries on the basis of their performance in social indicators like literacy and education levels, life expectancy and maternal mortality rates. This measure is called the Human Development Index.
- According to this conception development should be a process which allows more and more people to make meaningful choices and the pre-condition for this is the fulfilment of basic needs like food, education, health and shelter. This is called the basic needs approach.
- Popular slogans like 'roti, kapda aur makaan', 'garibi hatao' or 'bijli, sadak, pani' convey the sentiment that without the fulfilment of basic needs, it is impossible for an individual to live a dignified life and pursue her desires.
- Freedom from want or deprivation is the key to effectively exercising one's choices and pursuing one's desires.
- If people die of starvation or cold due to lack of food and shelter, or if children are working instead of being in school, this is indicative of a state of under-development.

DEVELOPMENT AND LIFESTYLE

- An alternative model of development would also try to move away from the high cost, ecologically wasteful, technology driven notion of development.

- Development should be measured the quality of life enjoyed by people in terms of happiness and harmony and satisfaction of essential needs.

- At one level, efforts should be made to conserve natural resources and use renewable sources of energy as far as is possible.

- Efforts such as rainwater harvesting, solar and bio-gas plants, micro-hydel projects, compost pits to generate manure out of organic waste are examples in this direction.

- Such activities have to take place at a local level and therefore demand higher involvement from people.

- At another level, there is also a need to scale down our need for non-renewable resources by changing lifestyles.

- However, any such policy would call for a high degree of co-operation between governments and people across countries.

- This would mean adopting democratic methods of decision-making on such matters.

23 Contemporary World Politics

THE COLD WAR ERA

- The Cold War referred to the competition, the tensions and a series of confrontations between the United States and Soviet Union, backed by their respective allies.

- The western alliance, headed by the US, represented the ideology of liberal democracy and capitalism while the eastern alliance, headed by the Soviet Union, was committed to the ideology of socialism and communism.

- **Cold War:** In 1945, the Allied Forces, led by the US, Soviet Union, Britain and France defeated the Axis Powers led by Germany, Italy and Japan, ending the Second World War (1939-1945). The war had involved almost all the major powers of the world and spread out to regions outside Europe including Southeast Asia, China, Burma (now Myanmar) and parts of India's northeast. The end of the Second World War was also the beginning of the Cold War. The world war ended when the United States dropped two atomic bombs on the Japanese cities of Hiroshima and Nagasaki in August 1945, causing Japan to surrender. While the Cold War was an outcome of the emergence of the US and the USSR as two superpowers rival to each other, it was also rooted in the understanding that the destruction caused by the use of atom bombs is too costly for any country to bear.

- **The Emergence of Two Power Blocs:** The alliance systems led by the two superpowers, therefore, threatened to divide the entire world into two camps. This division happened first in Europe. Most countries of Western Europe sided with the US and those of Eastern Europe joined the Soviet camp. That is why these were also called the 'western' and the 'eastern' alliances. The western alliance was formalised into an organisation, the North Atlantic Treaty Organisation (NATO), which came into existence in April 1949. It was an association of twelve states which declared that armed attack on any one of them in Europe or North America would be regarded as an attack on all of them. Each of these states would be obliged to help the other. The eastern alliance, known as the Warsaw Pact, was led by the Soviet Union. It was created in 1955 and its principal function was to counter NATO's forces in Europe. In East and Southeast Asia and in West Asia (Middle East), the United States built an alliance system called - the Southeast Asian Treaty Organisation (SEATO) and the Central Treaty

Organisation (CENTO). The Soviet Union and communist China responded by having close relations with regional countries such as North Vietnam, North Korea and Iraq.

- The roots of NAM went back to the friendship between three leaders - Yugoslavia's Josip Broz Tito, India's Jawaharlal Nehru, and Egypt's leader Gamal Abdel Nasser - who held a meeting in 1956. Indonesia's Sukarno and Ghana's Kwame Nkrumah strongly supported them. These five leaders came to be known as the five founders of NAM. The first non-aligned summit was held in Belgrade in 1961.

- The policy of staying away from alliances should not be considered isolationism or neutrality. Non-alignment is not isolationism since isolationism means remaining aloof from world affairs. Isolationism sums up the foreign policy of the US from the American War of Independence in 1787 up to the beginning of the First World War. In comparison, the non-aligned countries, including India, played an active role in mediating between the two rival alliances in the cause of peace and stability. Their strength was based on their unity and their resolve to remain non-aligned despite the attempt by the two superpowers to bring them into their alliances. Non-alignment is also not neutrality. Neutrality refers principally to a policy of staying out of war. States practicing neutrality are not required to help end a war. They do not get involved in wars and do not take any position on the appropriateness or morality of a war. Non-aligned states, including India, were actually involved in wars for various reasons. They also worked to prevent war between others and tried to end wars that had broken out.

Soviet System

- The Union of Soviet Socialist Republics (USSR) came into being after the socialist revolution in Russia in 1917. The revolution was inspired by the ideals of socialism, as opposed to capitalism, and the need for an egalitarian society. After the Second World War, the east European countries that the Soviet army had liberated from the fascist forces came under the control of the USSR. The political and the economic systems of all these countries were modelled after the USSR. This group of countries was called the Second World or the 'socialist bloc'. The Warsaw Pact, a military alliance, held them together. The USSR was the leader of the bloc. The Soviet state ensured a minimum standard of living for all citizens, and the government subsidised basic necessities including health, education, childcare and other welfare schemes. There was no unemployment. State ownership was the dominant form of ownership: land and productive assets were owned and controlled by the Soviet state. The Soviet system, however, became very bureaucratic and authoritarian, making life very difficult for its citizens. The Soviet Union lagged behind the West in technology, infrastructure (e.g., transport, power), and most importantly, in fulfilling the political or economic aspirations of citizens. The Soviet invasion of Afghanistan in 1979 weakened the system even further. The Soviet economy was faltering in the late 1970s and became stagnant.

- **Joseph Stalin (1879-1953):** Successor to Lenin and led the Soviet Union during its consolidation (1924-53); began rapid industrialization and forcible collectivisation of agriculture; credited with Soviet victory in the Second World War; held responsible for the Great Terror of the 1930s, authoritarian functioning and elimination of rivals within the party.

- In December 1991, under the leadership of Yeltsin, Russia, Ukraine and Belarus, three major republics of the USSR, declared that the Soviet Union was disbanded. The Communist Party of the Soviet Union was banned. Capitalism and democracy were adopted as the bases for the post-Soviet republics. The declaration on the disintegration of the USSR and the formation of the Commonwealth of Independent States (CIS) came as a surprise to the other republics, especially to the Central Asian ones. The exclusion of these republics was an issue that was quickly solved by making them founding members of the CIS. Russia was now accepted as the successor state of the Soviet Union. It inherited the Soviet seat in the UN Security Council. Russia accepted all the international treaties and commitments of the Soviet Union. It took over as the only nuclear state of the post- Soviet space and carried out some nuclear disarmament measures with the US. The old Soviet Union was thus dead and buried.

- The internal weaknesses of Soviet political and economic institutions, which failed to meet the aspirations of the people, were responsible for the collapse of the system. Economic stagnation for many years led to severe consumer shortages and a large section of Soviet society began to doubt and question the system and to do so openly.

- The Soviet Union had become stagnant in an administrative and political sense as well. The Communist Party that had ruled the Soviet Union for over 70 years was not accountable to the people. Ordinary people were alienated by slow and stifling administration, rampant corruption, the inability of the system to correct mistakes it had made, the unwillingness to allow more openness in government, and the centralization of authority in a vast land. Worse still, the party bureaucrats gained more privileges than ordinary citizens. People did not identify with the system and with the rulers, and the government increasingly lost popular backing.

- The rise of nationalism and the desire for sovereignty within various republics including Russia and the Baltic Republics (Estonia, Latvia and Lithuania), Ukraine, Georgia, and others proved to be the final and most immediate cause for the disintegration of the USSR.

Shock Therapy in Post-communist Regimes

- The collapse of communism was followed in most of these countries by a painful process of transition from an authoritarian socialist system to a democratic capitalist system. The model of transition in Russia, Central Asia and east Europe that was influenced by the World Bank and the IMF came to be known as 'shock therapy'. Each of these countries was required to make a total shift to a capitalist economy, which meant rooting out completely any structures evolved during the Soviet period. Above all, it meant that private ownership was to be the dominant pattern of ownership of property. Privatisation of state assets and corporate ownership patterns were to be immediately brought in. Collective farms were to be replaced by private farming and capitalism in agriculture. This transition ruled out any alternate or 'third way', other than state-controlled socialism or capitalism. Shock therapy also involved a drastic change in the external orientation of these economies. The free trade regime and foreign direct investment (FDI) were to be the main engines of change. This also involved openness to foreign investment, financial opening up or deregulation, and currency convertibility. Finally, the transition also involved a breakup of the existing trade alliances among the countries of the Soviet bloc. Each state from this bloc was now linked directly to the West and not to each other in the region. These states were thus to be gradually absorbed into the Western economic system.

Consequences of Shock Therapy

- In Russia, the large state-controlled industrial complex almost collapsed, as about 90 per cent of its industries were put up for sale to private individuals and companies. Since the restructuring was carried out through market forces and not by government-directed industrial policies, it led to the virtual disappearance of entire industries. This was called 'the largest garage sale in history', as valuable industries were undervalued and sold at throwaway prices. The value of the ruble, the Russian currency, declined dramatically. The rate of inflation was so high that people lost all their savings. The collective farm system disintegrated leaving people without food security, and Russia started to import food. The real GDP of Russia in 1999 was below what it was in 1989. The old trading structure broke down with no alternative in its place. The old system of social welfare was systematically destroyed. The withdrawal of government subsidies pushed large sections of the people into poverty. The middle classes were pushed to the periphery of society, and the academic and intellectual manpower disintegrated or migrated. A mafia emerged in most of these countries and started controlling many economic activities. The construction of democratic institutions was not given the same attention and priority as the demands of economic transformation. The constitutions of all these countries were drafted in a hurry and most, including Russia, had a strong executive president with the widest possible powers that rendered elected parliaments relatively weak. In Central Asia, the presidents had great powers, and several of them became very authoritarian.

- Most of these economies, especially Russia, started reviving in 2000, ten years after their independence. The reason for the revival for most of their economies was the export of natural resources like oil, natural gas and minerals. Azerbaijan, Kazakhstan, Russia, Turkmenistan and Uzbekistan are major oil and gas producers. Other countries have gained because of the oil pipelines that cross their territories for which they get rent.

- In Russia, two republics, Chechnya and Dagestan, have had violent secessionist movements. Moscow's method of dealing with the Chechen rebels and indiscriminate military bombings have led to many human rights violations but failed to deter the aspirations for independence.

- In Central Asia, Tajikistan witnessed a civil war that went on for ten years till 2001. The region as a whole has many sectarian conflicts. In Azerbaijan's province of Nagorno- Karabakh, some local Armenians want to secede and join Armenia. In Georgia, the demand for independence has come from two provinces, resulting in a civil war. There are movements against the existing regimes in Ukraine, Kyrgyzstan and Georgia. Countries and provinces are fighting over river waters.

- In Eastern Europe, Czechoslovakia split peacefully into two, with the Czechs and the Slovaks forming independent countries. But the most severe conflict took place in the Balkan republics of Yugoslavia. After 1991, it broke apart with several provinces like Croatia, Slovenia and Bosnia and Herzegovina declaring independence. Ethnic Serbs opposed this, and a massacre of non-Serb Bosnians followed. The NATO intervention and the bombing of Yugoslavia followed the inter-ethnic civil war.

India and Post-communist Countries

- India has maintained good relations with all the post-communist countries. Russia and India share a vision of a multipolar world order. What they mean by a multipolar world order is the co-existence of several powers in the international system, collective security (in which an attack on any country is regarded as a threat to all countries and requires a collective response), greater regionalism, negotiated settlements of international conflicts, an independent foreign policy for all countries, and decision making through bodies like the UN that should be strengthened, democratised, and empowered. More than 80 bilateral agreements have been signed between India and Russia as part of the Indo-Russian Strategic Agreement of 2001. India is seeking to increase its energy imports from Russia and the republics of Kazakhstan and Turkmenistan.

- The Soviet Union assisted India's public sector companies at a time when such assistance was difficult to get. It gave aid and technical assistance for steel plants like Bhilai, Bokaro, Visakhapatnam, and machinery plants like Bharat Heavy Electricals Ltd., etc. The Soviet Union accepted Indian currency for trade when India was short of foreign exchange.

- The Soviet Union supported India's positions on the Kashmir issue in the UN. It also supported India during its major conflicts, especially during the war with Pakistan in 1971.

US HEGEMONY IN WORLD POLITICS

- The US hegemony began in 1991 after Soviet power disappeared from the international scene.
- In August 1990, Iraq invaded Kuwait, rapidly occupying and subsequently annexing it. After a series of diplomatic attempts failed at convincing Iraq to quit its aggression, the United Nations mandated the liberation of Kuwait by force. For the UN, this was a dramatic decision after years of deadlock during the Cold War. The US President George H.W. Bush hailed the emergence of a 'new world order'. A massive coalition force of 660,000 troops from 34 countries fought against Iraq and defeated it in what came to be known as the First Gulf War. UN operation, which was called 'Operation Desert Storm', was overwhelmingly American. The First Gulf War revealed the vast technological gap that had opened up between the US military capability and that of other states. The highly publicised use of so called 'smart bombs' by the US led some observers to call this a 'computer war'. Widespread television coverage also made it a 'video game war', with viewers around the world watching the destruction of Iraqi forces live on TV in the comfort of their living rooms.

Despite winning the First Gulf War, George H.W. Bush lost the US presidential elections of 1992 to William Jefferson (Bill) Clinton of the Democratic Party. Bill Clinton won again in 1996 and thus remained the president of the US for eight years. In foreign policy, the

Clinton government tended to focus on 'soft issues' like democracy promotion, climate change and world trade rather than on the 'hard politics' of military power and security. In 1999, in response to Yugoslavian actions against the predominantly Albanian population in the province of Kosovo. The air forces of the NATO countries, led by the US, bombarded targets around Yugoslavia for well over two months, forcing the downfall of the government of Slobodan Milosevic and the stationing of a NATO force in Kosovo. Another significant US military action during the Clinton years was in response to the bombing of the US embassies in Nairobi, Kenya and Dar- es-Salaam, Tanzania in 1998. These bombings were attributed to Al-Qaeda, a terrorist organisation strongly influenced by extremist Islamist ideas. Within a few days of this bombing, President Clinton ordered Operation Infinite Reach, a series of cruise missile strikes on Al- Qaeda terrorist targets in Sudan and Afghanistan.

- **9/11 and the 'Global War on Terror** : On 11 September 2001, nineteen hijackers hailing from a number of Arab countries took control of four American commercial aircraft shortly after takeoff and flew them into important buildings in the US. One airliner each crashed into the North and South Towers of the World Trade Centre in New York. A third aircraft crashed into the Pentagon building in Arlington, Virginia, where the US Defence Department is headquartered. The fourth aircraft, presumably bound for the Capitol building of the US Congress, came down in a field in Pennsylvania. The attacks have come to be known as "9/11". The attacks killed nearly three thousand persons. In terms of their shocking effect on Americans, they have been compared to the British burning of Washington, DC in 1814 and the Japanese attack on Pearl Harbour in 1941. However, in terms of loss of life, 9/ 11 was the most severe attack on US soil since the founding of the country in 1776. As a part of its 'Global War on Terror', the US launched 'Operation Enduring Freedom' against all those suspected to be behind this attack, mainly Al-Qaeda and the Taliban regime in Afghanistan. The US forces made arrests all over the world, often without the knowledge of the government of the persons being arrested, transported these persons across countries and detained them in secret prisons. Some of them were brought to Guantanamo Bay, a US Naval base in Cuba, where the prisoners did not enjoy the protection of international law or the law of their own country or that of the US. Even the UN representatives were not allowed to meet these prisoners.

- On 19 March 2003, the US launched its invasion of Iraq under the codename 'Operation Iraqi Freedom'. More than forty other countries joined in the US-led 'coalition of the willing' after the UN refused to give its mandate to the invasion. The ostensible purpose of the invasion was to prevent Iraq from developing weapons of mass destruction (WMD). Since no evidence of WMD has been unearthed in Iraq, it is speculated that the invasion was motivated by other objectives, such as controlling Iraqi oilfields and installing a regime friendly to the US.

- The US share of the world economy remains an enormous 21 per cent. The US also accounts for almost 14 per cent of world trade, if intra-European Union trade is included in world trade data.

- The Bretton Woods system, set up by the US after the Second World War, still constitutes the basic structure of the world economy.

- The World Bank, International Monetary Fund (IMF) and World Trade Organisation (WTO) as the products of American hegemony.

- **India's Relationship with the US:** After the collapse of the Soviet Union, India suddenly found itself friendless in an increasingly hostile international environment. However, these were also the years when India decided to liberalise its economy and integrate it with the global economy. This policy and India's impressive economic growth rates in recent years have made the country an attractive economic partner for a number of countries including the US. The US absorbs about 65 per cent of India's total exports in the software sector. 35 per cent of the technical staff of Boeing is estimated to be of Indian origin. 300,000 Indians work in Silicon Valley. 15 percent of all high-tech start-ups are by Indian-Americans.

ALTERNATIVE CENTRES OF POWER

- **European Union:** In 1945, the European states confronted the ruin of their economies and the destruction of the assumptions and structures on which Europe had been founded. European integration after 1945 was aided by the Cold War. America extended massive financial help for reviving Europe's economy under what was called the 'Marshall Plan'. The US also created a new collective security structure under NATO. Under the Marshall Plan, the Organisation for European Economic Cooperation (OEEC) was established in 1948 to channel aid to the west European states. It became a forum where the western European states began to cooperate on trade and economic issues. The Council of Europe, established in 1949, was another step forward in political cooperation. The process of economic integration of European capitalist countries proceeded step by step leading to the formation of the European Economic Community in 1957. This process acquired a political dimension with the creation of the European Parliament. The collapse of the Soviet bloc put Europe on a fast track and resulted in the establishment of the European Union in 1992. The foundation was thus laid for a common foreign and security policy, cooperation on justice and home affairs, and the creation of a single currency. The EU has economic, political and diplomatic, and military influence. The EU is the world's second biggest economy with a GDP of more than $17 trillion in 2016, next to that of the United States of America. Its currency, the euro, can pose a threat to the dominance of the US dollar. Its share of world trade is much larger than that of the United States allowing it to be more assertive in trade disputes with the US and China. Its economic power gives it influence over its closest neighbours as well as in Asia and Africa. It also functions as an important bloc in international of the EU, France, holds permanent seat on the UN Security Council. The EU includes several non-permanent members of the UNSC. Militarily, the EU's combined armed forces are the second largest in the world. Its total spending on defence is second after the US. Two EU member states, Britain and France, also have nuclear arsenals of approximately 550 nuclear warheads. It is also the world's second most important source of space and communications technology. As a supranational organisation, the EU is able to intervene in economic, political and social areas. But in many areas its member states have their own foreign relations and defence policies that are often at odds with each other. Thus, Britain's Prime Minister Tony Blair was America's partner in the Iraq invasion, and many of the EU's newer members made up the US led 'coalition of the willing' whereas Germany and France opposed American policy. There is also a deep-seated 'Euroskepticism' in some parts of Europe about the EU's integrationist agenda. Thus, for example, Britain's former Prime Minister, Margaret Thatcher, kept the UK out of the European Market. Denmark and Sweden have resisted the Maastricht Treaty and the adoption of the euro, the common European currency. This limits the ability of the EU to act in matters of foreign relations and defence.

- **Association of South East Asian Nations (ASEAN):** ASEAN was established in 1967 by five countries of this region - Indonesia, Malaysia, the Philippines, Singapore and Thailand - by signing the Bangkok Declaration. The objectives of ASEAN were primarily to accelerate economic growth and through that 'social progress and cultural development'. A secondary objective was to promote regional peace and stability based on the rule of law and the principles of the United Nations Charter. Over the years, Brunei Darussalam, Vietnam, Lao PDR, Myanmar (Burma) and Cambodia joined ASEAN taking its strength to ten. ASEAN countries have celebrated what has become known as the 'ASEAN Way', a form of interaction that is informal, non-confrontationist and cooperative. The respect for national sovereignty is critical to the functioning of ASEAN. With some of the fastest growing economies in the world, ASEAN broadened its objectives beyond the economic and social spheres. In 2003, ASEAN moved along the path of the EU by agreeing to establish an ASEAN Community comprising three pillars, namely, the ASEAN Security Community, the ASEAN Economic Community and the ASEAN Socio- Cultural Community. The ASEAN security community was based on the conviction that outstanding territorial disputes should not escalate into armed confrontation. By 2003, ASEAN had several agreements in place by which member states promised to uphold peace, neutrality, cooperation, non-interference, and respect for national differences and sovereign rights. The ASEAN Regional Forum (ARF), which was established in 1994, is the organisation that carries out coordination of security and foreign policy. ASEAN was and still remains principally an economic association. The objectives of the ASEAN Economic Community are to create a common market and production base within ASEAN states and to aid social and economic development in the region. The Economic Community would also like to improve the existing ASEAN Dispute Settlement Mechanism to resolve economic disputes. ASEAN has focused on creating a Free Trade Area (FTA) for investment, labour, and services. The US and China have already moved fast to negotiate FTAs with ASEAN. Its Vision 2020 has defined an outward- looking role for ASEAN in the international community. This builds on the existing ASEAN policy to encourage negotiation over conflicts in the region. Thus, ASEAN has mediated the end of the Cambodian conflict, the East Timor crisis, and meets annually to discuss East Asian cooperation. India signed trade agreements with three ASEAN members, Malaysia, Singapore and Thailand. The ASEAN-India FTA came into effect in 2010.

- **The Rise of the Chinese Economy:** China's economic success since 1978 has been linked to its rise as a great power. China has been the fastest growing economy since the reforms first began there. It is projected to overtake the US as the world's largest economy by 2040. After the inception of the People's Republic of China in 1949, following the communist revolution under the leadership of Mao, its economy was based on the Soviet model. The economically backward communist China chose to sever its links with the capitalist world. It had little choice but to fall back on its own resources and, for a brief period, on Soviet aid and advice. The model was to create a state- owned heavy industries sector from the capital accumulated from agriculture. As it was short of foreign exchange that it needed in order to buy technology and goods on the world market, China decided to substitute imports by domestic goods. This model allowed China to use its resources to establish the foundations of an industrial economy on a scale that did not exist before. Employment and social welfare was assured to all citizens, and China moved ahead of most developing countries in educating its citizens and ensuring better health for them. The economy also grew at a respectable rate of 5-6 per cent. But an annual growth of 2-3 per cent in population meant that economic growth was insufficient to meet the needs of a growing population. Agricultural production was not sufficient to generate a surplus for industry. The Chinese leadership took major policy decisions in the 1970s. China ended its political and economic isolation with the establishment of relations with the United States in 1972. Premier Zhou Enlai proposed the 'four modernisations' (agriculture, industry, science and technology and military) in 1973. By 1978, the then leader Deng Xiaoping announced the 'open door' policy and economic reforms in China. The policy was to generate higher productivity by investments of capital and technology from abroad. The privatisation of agriculture in 1982 was followed by the privatisation of industry in 1998. Trade barriers were eliminated only in Special Economic Zones (SEZs) where foreign investors could set up enterprises. In China, the state played and continues to play a central role in setting up a market economy. Privatisation of agriculture led to a remarkable rise in agricultural production and rural incomes. High personal savings in the rural economy lead to an exponential growth in rural industry. The Chinese economy, including both industry and agriculture, grew at a faster rate. The new trading laws and the creation of Special Economic Zones led to a phenomenal rise in foreign trade. China has become the most important destination for foreign direct investment (FDI) anywhere in the world. It has large foreign exchange reserves that now allow it to make big investment in other countries. China's accession to the WTO in 2001 has been a further step in its opening to the outside world. While the Chinese economy has improved dramatically, not everyone in China has received the benefits of the reforms. Unemployment has risen in China with nearly 100 million people looking for jobs. Female employment and conditions of work are as bad as in Europe of the eighteenth and nineteenth centuries. Environmental degradation and corruption have increased besides a rise in economic inequality between rural and urban residents and coastal and inland provinces.

- **India–China Relations:** After India regained its independence from Britain, and China expelled the foreign powers, there was hope that both would come together to shape the future of the developing world and of Asia particularly. For a brief while, the slogan of 'Hindi-Chini bhaibhai' was popular. However, military conflict over a border dispute between the two countries marred that hope. Soon after independence, both states were involved in differences arising from the Chinese takeover of Tibet in 1950 and the final settlement of the Sino-Indian border. China and India were involved in a border conflict in 1962 over competing territorial claims principally in Arunachal Pradesh and in the Aksai Chin region of Ladakh. A series of talks to resolve the border issue were also initiated in 1981. Rajiv Gandhi's visit to China in December 1988 provided the impetus for an improvement in India-China relations. Since then both governments have taken measures to contain conflict and maintain 'peace and tranquillity' on the border. They have also signed agreements on cultural exchanges and cooperation in science and technology, and opened four border posts for trade. With India-China trade growing at 30 per cent per year since 1999, a more positive perspective on relations with China has emerged. Bilateral trade between India and China has increased from $338 million in 1992 to more than $84 billion in 2017. Recently the relation between the two countries has taken a downslide. Border disputes, China-Pakistan economic corridor and China's support to Pakistan in UN against India's move to counter terrorism are some of the factors for it.

- **Japan:** Japan has very few natural resources and imports most of its raw materials. Even then it progressed rapidly after the end of the Second World War. Japan became a member of the Organisation for Economic Cooperation and Development (OECD) in 1964. In 2017, it is the third largest economy in the world. It is the only Asian member of the G-7. It is the eleventh most populous nation in the world. Japan is the only nation that suffered the destruction caused by nuclear bombs. It is the second largest contributor to the regular budget of the UN, contributing almost 10 per cent of the total. Japan has a security alliance with the US since 1951. As per Article 9 of the Japanese Constitution, "the Japanese people forever renounce war as a sovereign right of the nation and the threat or use of force as means of settling international disputes." Although Japan's military expenditure is only one per cent of its GDP, it is the seventh largest in the world.

- **South Korea:** The Korean peninsula was divided into South Korea (Republic of Korea) and North Korea (Democratic People's Republic of Korea) at the end of the Second World War along the 38th Parallel. The Korean War during 1950-53 and dynamics of the Cold War era further intensified the rivalries between the two sides. Both the Koreas finally became Members of the UN on 17 September 1991. Meanwhile, South Korea emerged as a centre of power in Asia. Between the 1960s and the 1980s, it rapidly developed into an economic power, which is termed as "Miracle on the Han River". Signalling its all- round development, South Korea became a Member of the OECD in 1996. In 2017, its economy is the eleventh largest in the world and its military expenditure is the tenth largest. According to the Human Development Report 2016, the HDI rank of South Korea is 18. The major factors responsible for its high human development include "successful land reforms, rural development, extensive human resources development and rapid equitable economic growth." Other factors are export orientation, strong redistribution policies, public infrastructure development, effective institutions and governance. The South Korean brands such as Samsung, LG and Hyundai have become renowned in India. Numerous agreements between India and South Korea signify their growing commercial and cultural ties.

CONTEMPORARY SOUTH ASIA

- The expression 'South Asia' usually includes the following countries: Bangladesh, Bhutan, India, the Maldives, Nepal, Pakistan and Sri Lanka. The mighty Himalayas in the north and the vast Indian Ocean, the Arabian Sea and the Bay of Bengal in the south, west and east respectively provide a natural insularity to the region, which is largely responsible for the linguistic, social and cultural distinctiveness of the subcontinent. The boundaries of the region are not as clear in the east and the west, as they are in the north and the south. Afghanistan and Myanmar are often included in discussions of the region as a whole. China is an important player but is not considered to be a part of the region.

- The various countries in South Asia do not have the same kind of political systems. Despite many problems and limitations, Sri Lanka and India have successfully operated a democratic system since their independence from the British. Pakistan and Bangladesh have experienced both civilian and military rulers, with Bangladesh remaining a democracy in the post-Cold War period. Pakistan began the post- Cold War period with successive democratic governments under Benazir Bhutto and Nawaz Sharif respectively. But it suffered a military coup in 1999. It has been run by a civilian government again since 2008. Till 2006, Nepal was a constitutional monarchy with the danger of the king taking over executive powers. In 2008, the monarchy was abolished and Nepal emerged as a democratic republic. Bhutan became a constitutional monarchy in 2008. Under the leadership of the king, it emerged as a multi-party democracy. The Maldives, the other island nation, was a Sultanate till 1968 when it was transformed into a republic with a presidential form of government. In June 2005, the parliament of the Maldives voted unanimously to introduce a multiparty system. The Maldivian Democratic Party (MDP) dominates the political affairs of the island. The MDP won the 2018 Elections.

- **The Military Democracy in Pakistan:** After Pakistan framed its first constitution; General Ayub Khan took over the administration of the country and soon got himself elected. He had to give up office when there was popular dissatisfaction against his rule. This gave way to a military takeover once again under General Yahya Khan. During Yahya's military rule, Pakistan faced the Bangladesh crisis, and after a war with India in 1971, East Pakistan broke away to emerge as an independent country called Bangladesh. After this, an elected government under the leadership of Zulfikar Al Bhutto came to power in Pakistan from 1971 to 1977. The Bhutto government was removed by General Zia-ul-Haq in 1977. General Zia faced a pro- democracy movement from 1982 onwards and an elected democratic government was established once again in 1988 under the leadership of Benazir Bhutto. This phase of elective democracy lasted till 1999 when the army stepped in again and General Pervez Musharraf removed Prime Minister Nawaz Sharif. In 2001, General Musharraf got himself elected as the President. Since 2008, democratically elected leaders have been ruling Pakistan. The social dominance of the military, clergy, and landowning aristocracy has led to the frequent overthrow of elected governments and the establishment of military government. Pakistan's conflict with India has made the pro-military groups more powerful.

- **Democracy in Bangladesh:** Bangladesh was a part of Pakistan from 1947 to 1971. It consisted of the partitioned areas of Bengal and Assam from British India. The people of this region resented the domination of western Pakistan and the imposition of the Urdu language. Sheikh Mujibur Rahman led the popular struggle against West Pakistani domination. He demanded autonomy for the eastern region. In the 1970 elections in the then Pakistan, the Awami League led by Sheikh Mujib won all the seats in East Pakistan and secured a majority in the proposed constituent assembly for the whole of Pakistan. But the government dominated by the West Pakistani leadership refused to convene the assembly. Sheikh Mujib was arrested. Under the military rule of General Yahya Khan, the Pakistani army tried to suppress the mass movement of the Bengali people. Thousands were killed by the Pakistan army. This led to a large scale migration into India, creating a huge refugee problem for India. The government of India supported the demand of the people of East Pakistan for their independence and helped them financially and militarily. This resulted in a war between India and Pakistan in December 1971 that ended in the surrender of the Pakistani forces in East Pakistan and the formation of Bangladesh as an independent country. Bangladesh drafted its constitution declaring faith in secularism, democracy and socialism. However, in 1975 Sheikh Mujib got the constitution amended to shift from the parliamentary to presidential form of government. He also abolished all parties except his own, the Awami League. He was assassinated in a military uprising in August 1975. The new military ruler, Ziaur Rahman, formed his own Bangladesh National Party and won elections in 1979. He was assassinated and another military takeover followed under the leadership of Lt Gen H. M. Ershad. Since 1999 representative democracy based on multi-party elections has been working in Bangladesh.

- **Monarchy and Democracy in Nepal:** Nepal was a Hindu kingdom in the past and then a constitutional monarchy in the modern period for many years. During the nineties, the Maoists of Nepal were successful in spreading their influence in many parts of Nepal. They believed in armed insurrection against the monarch and the ruling elite. This led to a violent conflict between the Maoist guerrillas and the armed forces of the king. For some time, there was a triangular conflict among the monarchist forces, the democrats and the Maoists. In 2002, the king abolished the parliament and dismissed the government, thus ending even the limited democracy that existed in Nepal. In 2008, Nepal became a democratic republic after abolishing the monarchy. In 2015, it adopted a new constitution.

- **Ethnic Conflict and Democracy in Sri Lanka:** After its independence in 1948 politics in Sri Lanka (it was then known as Ceylon) was dominated by forces that represented the interest of the majority Sinhala community. They were hostile to a large number of Tamils who had migrated from India to Sri Lanka and settled there. This migration continued even after independence. The Sinhala nationalists thought that Sri Lanka should not give 'concessions' to the Tamils because Sri Lanka belongs to the Sinhala people only. The neglect of Tamil concerns led to militant Tamil nationalism. From 1983 onwards, the militant organisation, the Liberation Tigers of Tamil Eelam (LTTE) has been fighting an armed struggle with the army of Sri Lanka and demanding 'Tamil Eelam' or a separate country for the Tamils of Sri Lanka. The LTTE controls the north-eastern parts of Sri Lanka. In 1987, the government of India for the first time got directly involved in the Sri Lankan Tamil question. India signed an accord with Sri Lanka and sent troops to stabilise relations between the Sri Lankan government and the Tamils. Eventually, the Indian Army got into a fight with the LTTE. The presence of Indian troops was also not liked much by the Sri Lankans. They saw this as an attempt by India to interfere in the internal affairs of Sri Lanka. In 1989, the Indian Peace Keeping Force (IPKF) pulled out of Sri Lanka without attaining its objective. The Sri Lankan crisis continued to be violent. However, international actors, particularly the Scandinavian countries such as Norway and Iceland tried to bring the warring groups back to negotiations. Finally, the armed conflict came to an end, as the LTTE was vanquished in 2009. Sri Lanka was one of the first developing countries to successfully control the rate of growth of population, the first country in the region to liberalise the economy, and it has had the highest per capita gross domestic product (GDP) for many years right through the civil war. Despite the ravages of internal conflict, it has maintained a democratic political system.

- **India-Pakistan Conflicts:** Soon after the partition, the two countries got embroiled in a conflict over the fate of Kashmir. The Pakistani government claimed that Kashmir belonged to it. Wars between India and Pakistan in 1947- 48 and 1965 failed to settle the matter. The 1947-48 war resulted in the division of the province into Pakistan- occupied Kashmir and the Indian province of Jammu and Kashmir divided by the Line of Control. In 1971, India won a decisive war against Pakistan but the Kashmir issue remained unsettled. India's conflict with Pakistan is also over strategic issues like the control of the Siachen glacier and over acquisition of arms. The arms race between the two countries assumed a new character with both states acquiring nuclear weapons and missiles to deliver such arms against each other in the 1990s. In 1998, India conducted nuclear explosion in Pokaran. Pakistan responded within a few days by carrying out nuclear tests in the Chagai Hills. The Indian government has blamed the Pakistan government for using a strategy of low-key violence by helping the Kashmiri militants with arms, training, money and protection to carry out terrorist strikes against India. The Indian government also believes that Pakistan had aided the pro-Khalistani militants with arms and ammunitions during the period 1985-1995. Its spy agency, Inter Services Intelligence (ISI), is alleged to be involved in various anti-India campaigns in India's northeast, operating secretly through Bangladesh and Nepal. In 1960, with the help of the World Bank, India and Pakistan signed the Indus Waters Treaty over the use of the rivers of the Indus basin. The two countries are not in agreement over the demarcation line in Sir Creek in the Rann of Kutch.

- **India and its Other Neighbours:** The governments of India and Bangladesh have had differences over several issues including the sharing of the Ganga and Brahmaputra river waters. The Indian government has been unhappy with Bangladesh's denial of illegal immigration to India, its support for anti-Indian Islamic fundamentalist groups, Bangladesh's refusal to allow Indian troops to move through its territory to north-eastern India, and its decision not to export natural gas to India or allow Myanmar to do so through Bangladeshi territory. Bangladesh is a part of India's Look East (Act East since 2014) policy that wants to link up with Southeast Asia via Myanmar. Nepal and India has a treaty between the two countries allows the citizens of the two countries to travel to and work in the other country without visas and passports. The Indian government has often expressed displeasure at the warm relationship between Nepal and China and at the Nepal government's inaction against anti- Indian elements. Indian security agencies see the Maoist movement in Nepal as a growing security threat, given the rise of Naxalite groups in various Indian states from Bihar in the north to Andhra Pradesh in the south. Many leaders and citizens in Nepal think that the Indian government interferes in its internal affairs, has designs on its river waters and hydro-electricity, and prevents Nepal, a landlocked country, from getting easier access to the sea through Indian Territory. India enjoys a very special relationship with Bhutan too and does not have any major conflict with the Bhutanese government. The efforts made by the Bhutanese monarch to weed out the guerrillas and militants from north-eastern India that operate in his country have been helpful to India. India is involved in big hydroelectric projects in Bhutan and remains the Himalayan kingdom's biggest source of development aid. India's ties with the Maldives remain warm and cordial. In November 1988, when some Tamil mercenaries from Sri Lanka attacked the Maldives, the Indian air force and navy reacted quickly to the Maldives' request to help stop the invasion. Nepal and Bhutan, as well as Bangladesh and Myanmar, have had disagreements in the past over the migration of ethnic Nepalese into Bhutan and the Rohingyas into Myanmar, respectively. Bangladesh and Nepal have had some differences over the future of the Himalayan river waters.

- **Peace and Cooperation:** The South Asian Association for Regional Cooperation (SAARC) is a major regional initiative by the South Asian states to evolve cooperation through multilateral means. It began in 1985. Unfortunately, due to persisting political differences, SAARC has not had much success. SAARC members signed the South Asian Free Trade (SAFTA) agreement which promised the formation of a free trade zone for the whole of South Asia. A new chapter of peace and cooperation might evolve in South Asia if all the countries in the region allow free trade across the borders. This is the spirit behind the idea of SAFTA. The Agreement was signed in 2004 and came into effect on 1 January 2006. SAFTA aims at lowering trade tariffs. China and the United States remain key players in South Asian politics. Sino-Indian relations have improved significantly in the last ten years, but China's strategic partnership with Pakistan remains a major irritant.

INTERNATIONAL ORGANISATIONS

- An international organisation is not a super-state with authority over its members. It is created by and responds to states. It comes into being when states agree to its creation. Once created, it can help member states resolve their problems peacefully.

- **IMF:** The International Monetary Fund (IMF) is an international organisation that oversees those financial institutions and regulations that act at the international level. The IMF has 189 member countries (as on 12 April 2016) but they do not enjoy an equal say. The G-7 members US (16.52%), Japan (6.15%), Germany (5.32%), France (4.03%), UK (4.03%), Italy (3.02%) and Canada (2.22%) have 41.29% of the votes. China (6.09%), India (2.64%), Russia (2.59%) Brazil (2.22%) and Saudi Arabia (2.02%) are the other major members.

- **Evolution of the UN:** The First World War encouraged the world to invest in an international organisation to deal with conflict. Many believed that such an organisation would help the world to avoid war. As a result, the League of Nations was born. However, despite its initial success, it could not prevent the Second World War (1939-45). The UN was founded as a successor to the League of Nations. It was established in 1945 immediately after the Second World War. The organisation was set up through the signing of the United Nations Charter by 51 states. The UN's objective is to prevent international conflict and to facilitate cooperation among states. By 2011, the UN had 193 member states. These included almost all independent states. In the UN General Assembly, all members have one vote each. In the UN Security Council, there are five permanent members. These are: the United States, Russia, the United Kingdom, France and China. These states were selected as permanent members as they were the most powerful immediately after the Second World War and because they constituted the victors in the War. The present Secretary-General is António Guterres. He is the ninth Secretary-General of the UN. He took over as the Secretary-General on 1 January 2017. He was the Prime Minister of Portugal (1995-2002) and the UN High Commissioner for Refugees (2005-2015).

- The UN consists of many different structures and agencies. War and peace and differences between member states are discussed in the General Assembly as well as the Security Council. Social and economic issues are dealt with by many agencies including the World Health Organisation (WHO), the United Nations Development Programme (UNDP), the United Nations Human Rights Commission (UNHRC), and the United Nations High Commission for Refugees (UNHCR), the United Nations Children's Fund (UNICEF), and the United Nations Educational, Scientific, and Cultural Organisation (UNESCO), among others.

- **World Bank:** The World Bank was created during the Second World War in 1944. Its activities are focused on the developing countries. It works for human development (education, health), agriculture and rural development (irrigation, rural services), environmental protection (pollution reduction, establishing and enforcing regulations), infrastructure (roads, urban regeneration, and electricity) and governance (anti-corruption, development of legal institutions). It provides loans and grants to the member-countries. In this way, it exercises enormous influence on the economic policies of developing countries. It is often criticised for setting the economic agenda of the poorer nations, attaching stringent conditions to its loans and forcing free market reforms.

- **WTO:** The World Trade Organisation (WTO) is an international organisation which sets the rules for global trade. This organisation was set up in 1995 as the successor to the General Agreement on Trade and Tariffs (GATT) created after the Second World War. It has 164 members (as on 29 July 2016). All decisions are taken unanimously but the major economic powers such as the US, EU and Japan has managed to use the WTO to frame rules of trade to advance their own interests. The developing countries often complain of non-transparent procedures and being pushed around by big powers.

- **IAEA:** The International Atomic Energy Agency (IAEA) was established in 1957. It came into being to implement US President Dwight Eisenhower's "Atoms for Peace" proposal. It seeks to promote the peaceful use of nuclear energy and to prevent its use for military purposes. IAEA teams regularly inspect nuclear facilities all over the world to ensure that civilian reactors are not being used for military purposes.

- **Amnesty International:** Amnesty International is an NGO that campaigns for the protection of human rights all over the world. It promotes respect for all the human rights in the Universal Declaration of Human Rights. It believes that human rights are interdependent and indivisible. It prepares and publishes reports on human rights. Governments are not always happy with these reports since a major focus of Amnesty is the misconduct of government authorities. Nevertheless, these reports play an important role in research and advocacy on human rights.

- **Human Rights Watch:** Human Rights Watch is another international NGO involved in research and advocacy on human rights. It is the largest international human rights organisation in the US. It draws the global media's attention to human rights abuses. It helped in building international coalitions like the campaigns to ban landmines, to stop the use of child soldiers and to establish the International Criminal Court.

SECURITY IN THE CONTEMPORARY WORLD

- **What is Security?:** At its most basic, security implies freedom from threats. Security relates only to extremely dangerous threats-threats that could so endanger core values that those values would be damaged beyond repair if we did not do something to deal with the situation.

- **Traditional Notions:** *External:* In the traditional conception of security, the greatest danger to a country is from military threats. The source of this danger is another country which by threatening military action endangers the core values of sovereignty, independence and territorial integrity. Military action also endangers the lives of ordinary citizens. Security policy is concerned with preventing war, which is called deterrence, and with limiting or ending war, which is called defence. Traditional security policy has a third component called balance of power. A good part of maintaining a balance of power is to build up one's military power, although economic and technological power are also important since they are the basis for military power. A fourth and related component of traditional security policy is alliance building. An alliance is a coalition of states that coordinate their actions to deter or defend against military attack. Most alliances are formalised in written treaties and are based on a fairly clear identification of who constitutes the threat. Countries form alliances to increase their effective power relative to another country or alliance. Alliances are based on national interests and can change when national interests change.

- **Internal:** Traditional security must also, therefore, concern itself with internal security. As the colonies became free from the late 1940s onwards, their security concerns were often similar to that of the European powers. Some of the newly independent countries, like the European powers, became members of the Cold War alliances. They, therefore, had to worry about the Cold War becoming a hot war and dragging them into hostilities - against neighbours who might have joined the other side in the Cold War, against the leaders of the alliances (the United States or Soviet Union), or against any of the other partners of the US and Soviet Union. The Cold War between the two superpowers was responsible for approximately one-third of all wars in the post-Second World War period. Most of these wars were fought in the Third World. Just as the European colonial powers feared violence in the colonies, some colonial people feared, after independence, that they might be attacked by their former colonial rulers in Europe. They had to prepare, therefore, to defend themselves against an imperial war. The security challenges facing the newly- independent countries of Asia and Africa were different from the challenges in Europe in two ways. For one thing, the new countries faced the prospect of military conflict with neighbouring countries. For another, they had to worry about internal military conflict. These countries faced threats not only from outside their borders, mostly from neighbours, but also from within. Many newly independent countries came to fear their neighbours even more than they feared the US or Soviet Union or the former colonial powers. They quarrelled over borders and territories or control of people and populations or all of these simultaneously. Internal wars now make up more than 95 per cent of all armed conflicts fought anywhere in the world. Between 1946 and 1991, there was a twelve-fold rise in the number of civil wars-the greatest jump in 200 years. So, for the new states, external wars with neighbours and internal wars posed a serious challenge to their security.

- **Traditional Security and Cooperation:** In traditional security, there is recognition that cooperation in limiting violence is possible. These limits relate both to the ends and the means of war. Traditional views of security do not rule out other forms of cooperation as well. The most important of these are disarmament, arms control, and confidence building. Disarmament requires all states to give up certain kinds of weapons. For example, the 1972 Biological Weapons Convention (BWC) and the 1992 Chemical Weapons Convention (CWC) banned the production and possession of these weapons. More than 155 states acceded to the BWC and 181 states acceded to the CWC. Both conventions included all the great powers. But the superpowers - the US and Soviet Union did not want to give up the third type of weapons of mass destruction, namely, nuclear weapons, so they pursued arms control. Arms control regulates the acquisition or development of weapons. The Anti-ballistic Missile (ABM) Treaty in 1972 tried to stop the United States and Soviet Union from using ballistic missiles as a defensive shield to launch a nuclear attack. While it did allow both countries to deploy a very limited number of defensive systems, it stopped them from large-scale production of those systems. The US and Soviet Union signed a number of other arms control treaties including the Strategic Arms Limitations Treaty II or SALT II and the Strategic Arms Reduction Treaty (START). The Nuclear Non-Proliferation Treaty (NPT) of 1968 was an arms control treaty in the sense that it regulated the acquisition of nuclear weapons: those countries that had tested and manufactured nuclear weapons before 1967 were allowed to keep their weapons; and those that had not done so were to give up the right to acquire them. The NPT did not abolish nuclear weapons; rather, it limited the number of countries that could have them. Traditional security also accepts confidence building as a means of avoiding violence. Confidence building is a process in which countries share ideas and information with their rivals. Confidence building is a process designed to ensure that rivals do not go to war through misunderstanding or misperception.

- **Non-Traditional Notions:** Non-traditional views of security have been called 'human security' or 'global security'. Human security is about the protection of people more than the protection of states. Human security and state security should be - and often are - the same thing. All proponents of human security agree that its primary goal is the protection of individuals. Proponents of the 'narrow' concept of human security focus on violent threats to individuals or, as former UN Secretary-General Kofi Annan puts it, "the protection of communities and individuals from internal violence". Proponents of the 'broad' concept of human security argue that the threat agenda should include hunger, disease and natural disasters because these kill far more people than war, genocide and terrorism combined. Human security policy, they argue, should protect people from these threats as well as from violence. In its broadest formulation, the human security agenda also encompasses economic security and 'threats to human dignity'. Put differently, the broadest formulation stresses what has been called 'freedom from want' and 'freedom from fear', respectively. The idea of global security emerged in the 1990s in response to the global nature of threats such as global warming, international terrorism, and health epidemics like AIDS and bird flu and so on.

- **New Sources of Threats:** Terrorism refers to political violence that targets civilians deliberately and indiscriminately. International terrorism involves the citizens or territory of more than one country. Terrorist groups seek to change a political context or condition that they do not like by force or threat of force. Civilian targets are usually chosen to terrorise the public and to use the unhappiness of the public as a weapon against national governments or other parties in conflict. The classic cases of terrorism involve hijacking planes or planting bombs in trains, cafes, markets and other crowded places. Since 11 September 2001 when terrorists attacked the World Trade Centre in America, other governments and public have paid more attention to terrorism, though terrorism itself is not new. In the past, most of the terror attacks have occurred in the Middle East, Europe, Latin America and South Asia.

- **Global poverty :** Global poverty is another source of insecurity. World population—now at 760 crore— will grow to nearly 1000 crore by the middle of the 21st century. Currently, half the world's population growth occurs in just six countries— India, China, Pakistan, Nigeria, Bangladesh and Indonesia. Among the world's poorest countries, population is expected to triple in the next 50 years, whereas many rich countries will see population shrinkage in that period. High per capita income and low population growth make rich states or rich social groups get richer, whereas low incomes and high population growth reinforce each other to make poor states and poor groups get poorer. Globally, this disparity contributes to the gap between the Northern and Southern countries of the world. Within the South, disparities have also sharpened, as a few countries have managed to slow down population growth and raise incomes while others have failed to do so. Poverty in the South has also led to large-scale migration to seek a better life, especially better economic opportunities, in the North. This has created international political frictions. International law and norms make a distinction between migrants (those who voluntarily leave their home countries) and refugees (those who flee from war, natural disaster or political persecution). States are generally supposed to accept refugees, but they do not have to accept migrants. While refugees leave their country of origin, people who have fled their homes but remain within national borders are called 'internally displaced people'. Kashmiri Pandits that fled the violence in the Kashmir Valley in the early 1990s are an example of an internally displaced community.

- **India's Security Strategy:** India has faced traditional (military) and non-traditional threats to its security that have emerged from within as well as outside its borders. Its security strategy has four broad components. The first component was strengthening its military capabilities because India has been involved in conflicts with its neighbours —Pakistan in 1947–48, 1965, 1971 and 1999; and China in 1962. Since it is surrounded by nuclear-armed countries in the South Asian region, India's decision to conduct nuclear tests in 1998 was justified by the Indian government in terms of safeguarding national security. India first tested a nuclear device in 1974. The second component of India's security strategy has been to strengthen international norms and international institutions to protect its security interests. India's first Prime Minister, Jawaharlal Nehru, supported the cause of Asian solidarity, decolonisation, disarmament, and the UN as a forum in which international conflicts could be settled. India also took initiatives to bring about a universal and non-discriminatory non- proliferation regime in which all countries would have the same rights and obligations with respect to weapons of mass destruction (nuclear, biological, chemical). It argued for an equitable New International Economic Order (NIEO). Most importantly, it used non-alignment to help carve out an area of peace outside the bloc politics of the two superpowers. India joined 160 countries that have signed and ratified the 1997 Kyoto Protocol, which provides a roadmap for reducing the emissions of greenhouse gases to check global warming. Indian troops have been sent abroad on UN peacekeeping missions in support of cooperative security initiatives. The third component of Indian security strategy is geared towards meeting security challenges within the country. Several militant groups from areas such as the Nagaland, Mizoram, the Punjab, and Kashmir among others have, from time to time, sought to break away from India. India has tried to preserve national unity by adopting a democratic political system, which allows different communities and groups of people to freely articulate their grievances and share political power. Finally, there has been an attempt in India to develop its economy in a way that the vast mass of citizens are lifted out of poverty and misery and huge economic inequalities are not allowed to exist.

ENVIRONMENTAL CONCERNS IN GLOBAL POLITICS

Throughout the world, cultivable area is barely expanding any more, and a substantial portion of existing agricultural land is losing fertility. Grasslands have been overgrazed and fisheries overharvested. Water bodies have suffered extensive depletion and pollution, severely restricting food production. According to the Human Development Report 2016 of the United Nations Development Programme, 663 million people in developing countries have no access to safe water and 2.4 billion have no access to sanitation, resulting in the death of more than three million children every year. Natural forests — which help stabilise the climate, moderate water supplies, and harbor a majority of the planet's biodiversity on land—are being cut down and people are being displaced. The loss of biodiversity continues due to the destruction of habitat in areas which are rich in species. A steady decline in the total amount of ozone in the Earth's stratosphere (commonly referred to as the ozone hole) poses a real danger to ecosystems and human health. Coastal pollution too is increasing globally. Although the open sea is relatively clean, the coastal waters are becoming increasingly polluted largely due to land-based activities. If unchecked, intensive human settlement of coastal zones across the globe will lead to further deterioration in the quality of marine environment. Although environmental concerns have a long history, awareness of the environmental consequences of economic growth acquired an increasingly political character from the 1960s onwards. The Club of Rome, a global think tank, published a book in 1972 entitled Limits to Growth, dramatising the potential depletion of the Earth's resources against the backdrop of rapidly growing world population. International agencies, including the United Nations Environment Programme (UNEP), began holding international conferences and promoting detailed studies to get a more coordinated and effective response to environmental problems. The growing focus on environmental issues within the arena of global politics was firmly consolidated at the United Nations Conference on Environment and Development held in Rio de Janeiro, Brazil, in June 1992. This was also called the Earth Summit. Five years earlier, the 1987 Brundtland Report, Our Common Future, had warned that traditional patterns of economic growth were not sustainable in the long term, especially in view of the demands of the South for further industrial development. What was obvious at the Rio Summit was that the rich and developed countries of the First World, generally referred to as the 'global North' were pursuing a different environmental agenda than the poor and developing countries of the Third World, called the 'global South'. Whereas the Northern states were concerned with ozone depletion and global warming, the Southern states were anxious to address the relationship between economic development and environmental management. The Rio Summit produced conventions dealing with climate change, biodiversity, forestry, and recommended a list of development practices called 'Agenda 21'. But it left unresolved considerable differences and difficulties. There was a consensus on combining economic growth with ecological responsibility. This approach to development is commonly known as 'sustainable development'.

INDIA'S STAND ON ENVIRONMENTAL ISSUES

India signed and ratified the 1997 Kyoto Protocol in August 2002. India, China and other developing countries were exempt from the requirements of the Kyoto Protocol because their contribution to the emission of greenhouse gases during the industrialisation period (that is believed to be causing today's global warming and climate change) was not significant. However, the critics of the Kyoto Protocol point out that sooner or later, both India and China, along with other developing countries, will be among the leading contributors to greenhouse gas emissions. At the G-8 meeting in June 2005, India pointed out that the per capita emission rates of the developing countries are a tiny fraction of those in the developed world. Following the principle of common but differentiated responsibilities, India is of the view that the major responsibility of curbing emission rests with the developed countries, which have accumulated emissions over a long period of time. India's international negotiating position relies heavily on principles of historical responsibility, as enshrined in UNFCCC. This acknowledges that developed countries are responsible for most historical and current greenhouse gas emissions, and emphasizes that 'economic and social development are the first and overriding priorities of the developing country parties'. So India is wary of recent discussions within UNFCCC about introducing binding commitments on rapidly industrialising countries (such as Brazil, China and India) to reduce their greenhouse gas emissions. India feels this contravenes the very spirit of UNFCCC. Neither does it seem fair to impose restrictions on India when the country's rise in per capita carbon emissions by 2030 is likely to still represent less than half the world average of 3.8 tonnes in 2000. Indian emissions are predicted to rise from 0.9 tonnes per capita in 2000 to 1.6 tonnes per capita in 2030. The Indian government is already participating in global efforts through a number of programmes. For example, India's National Auto-fuel Policy mandates cleaner fuels for vehicles. The Energy Conservation Act, passed in 2001, outlines initiatives to improve energy efficiency. Similarly, the Electricity Act of 2003 encourages the use of renewable energy. Recent trends in importing natural gas and encouraging the adoption of clean coal technologies show that India has been making real efforts. The government is also keen to launch a National Mission on Biodiesel, using about 11 million hectares of land to produce biodiesel by 2011–2012. India ratified the Paris Climate Agreement on 2 October 2016. And India has one of the largest renewable energy programmes in the world. A review of the implementation of the agreements at the Earth Summit in Rio was undertaken by India in 1997. One of the key conclusions was that there had been no meaningful progress with respect to transfer of new and additional financial resources and environmentally-sound technology on concessional terms to developing nations. India finds it necessary that developed countries take immediate measures to provide developing countries with financial resources and clean technologies to enable them to meet their existing commitments under UNFCCC. India is also of the view that the SAARC countries should adopt a common position on major global environment issues, so that the region's voice carries greater weight.

RESOURCE GEOPOLITICS

Resource geopolitics is all about who gets what, when, where and how. Resources have provided some of the key means and motives of global European power expansion. They have also been the focus of inter-state rivalry. Western geopolitical thinking about resources has been dominated by the relationship of trade, war and power, at the core of which were overseas resources and maritime navigation. Since sea power itself rested on access to timber, naval timber supply became a key priority for major European powers from the 17th century onwards. The critical importance of ensuring uninterrupted supply of strategic resources, in particular oil, was well established both during the First World War and the Second World War. Throughout the Cold War the industrialised countries of the North adopted a number of methods to ensure a steady flow of resources. Traditional Western strategic thinking remained concerned with access to supplies, which might be threatened by the Soviet Union. A particular concern was Western control of oil in the Gulf and strategic minerals in Southern and Central Africa. After the end of the Cold War and the disintegration of the Soviet Union, the security of supply continues to worry government and business decisions with regard to several minerals, in particular radioactive materials. However, oil continues to be the most important resource in global strategy. The global economy relied on oil for much of the 20th century as a portable and indispensable fuel. The immense wealth associated with oil generates political struggles to control it, and the history of petroleum is also the history of war and struggle. Nowhere is this more obviously the case than in West Asia and Central Asia. West Asia, specifically the Gulf region, accounts for about 30 per cent of global oil production. But it has about 64 percent of the planet's known reserves, and is therefore the only region able to satisfy any substantial rise in oil demand. Saudi Arabia has a quarter of the world's total reserves and is the single largest producer. Iraq's known reserves are second only to Saudi Arabia's. And, since substantial portions of Iraqi territory are yet to be fully explored, there is a fair chance that actual reserves might be far larger. The United States, Europe, Japan, and increasingly India and China, which consume this petroleum, are located at a considerable distance from the region. Water is another crucial resource that is relevant to global politics. Regional variations and the increasing scarcity of freshwater in some parts of the world point to the possibility of disagreements over shared water resources as a leading source of conflicts in the 21st century. Some commentators on world politics have referred to 'water wars' to describe the possibility of violent conflict over this life sustaining resource. Countries that share rivers can disagree over many things. For instance, a typical disagreement is a downstream (lower riparian) state's objection to pollution, excessive irrigation, or the construction of dams by an upstream (upper riparian) state, which might decrease or degrade the quality of water available to the downstream state. States have used force to protect or seize freshwater resources. Examples of violence include those between Israel, Syria, and Jordan in the 1950s and 1960s over attempts by each side to divert water from the Jordan and Yarmuk Rivers, and more recent threats between Turkey, Syria, and Iraq over the construction of dams on the Euphrates River. A number of studies show that countries that share rivers — and many countries do share rivers — are involved in military conflicts with each other.

24   Globalisation

INTRODUCTION

- Globalisation need not always be positive; it can have negative consequences for the people.

- Globalisation as a concept fundamentally deals with flows. These flows could be of various kinds — ideas moving from one part of the world to another, capital shunted between two or more places, commodities being traded across borders, and people moving in search of better livelihoods to different parts of the world. The crucial element is the 'worldwide interconnectedness' that is created and sustained as a consequence of these constant flows.

- Globalisation is a multidimensional concept. It has political, economic and cultural manifestations.

- The impact of globalisation is vastly uneven — it affects some societies more than others and some parts of some societies more than others.

CAUSES OF GLOBALISATION

- While globalisation is not caused by any single factor, technology remains a critical element. There is no doubt that the invention of the telegraph, the telephone, and the microchip in more recent times has revolutionised communication between different parts of the world.

Political Consequences

- Globalisation results in an erosion of state capacity, that is, the ability of government to do what they do. All over the world, the old 'welfare state' is now giving way to a more minimalist state that performs certain core functions such as the maintenance of law and order and the security of its citizens. However, it withdraws from many of its earlier welfare functions directed at economic and social well-being. In place of the welfare state, it is the market that becomes the prime determinant of economic and social priorities. The entry and the increased role of multinational companies all over the world lead to a reduction in the capacity of governments to take decisions on their own. State capacity has received a boost as a consequence of globalisation, with enhanced technologies available at the disposal of the state to collect information about its citizens. With this information, the state is better able to rule, not less able. Thus, states become more powerful than they were earlier as an outcome of the new technology.

Economic Consequences

* Economic globalisation draws our attention immediately to the role of international institutions like the IMF and the WTO and the role they play in determining economic policies across the world. Economic globalisation usually involves greater economic flows among different countries of the world. Some of this is voluntary and some forced by international institutions and powerful countries. Globalisation has involved greater trade in commodities across the globe; the restrictions imposed by different countries on allowing the imports of other countries have been reduced. Similarly, the restrictions on movement of capital across countries have also been reduced. In operational terms, it means that investors in the rich countries can invest their money in countries other than their own, including developing countries, where they might get better returns. Globalisation has also led to the flow of ideas across national boundaries. The spread of internet and computer related services are an example of that. But globalisation has not led to the same degree of increase in the movement of people across the globe. Developed countries have carefully guarded their borders with visa policies to ensure that citizens of other countries cannot take away the jobs of their own citizens. Globalisation has led to similar economic policies adopted by governments in different parts of the world, this has generated vastly different outcomes in different parts of the world. Economic globalisation has created an intense division of opinion all over the world. Those who are concerned about social justice are worried about the extent of state withdrawal caused by processes of economic globalisation. They point out that it is likely to benefit only a small section of the population while impoverishing those who were dependent on the government for jobs and welfare (education, health, sanitation, etc.). They have emphasised the need to ensure institutional safeguards or creating 'social safety nets' to minimise the negative effects of globalisation on those who are economically weak. Many movements all over the world feel that safety nets are insufficient or unworkable. They have called for a halt to forced economic globalisation, for its results would lead to economic ruin for the weaker countries, especially for the poor within these countries.

Cultural Consequences

* The cultural effect of globalisation leads to the fear that this process poses a threat to cultures in the world. It does so, because globalisation leads to the rise of a uniform culture or what is called cultural homogenisation. The rise of a uniform culture is not the emergence of a global culture. What we have in the name of a global culture is the imposition of Western culture on the rest of the world. While cultural homogenization is an aspect of globalisation, the same process also generates precisely the opposite effect. It leads to each culture becoming more different and distinctive. This phenomenon is called cultural heterogenisation.

INDIA AND GLOBALISATION

- During the colonial period, as a consequence of Britain's imperial ambitions, India became an exporter of primary goods and raw materials and a consumer of finished goods. After independence, because of this experience with the British, we decided to make things ourselves rather than relying on others. We also decided not to allow others to export to us so that our own producers could learn to make things. This 'protectionism' generated its own problems. While some advances were made in certain arenas, critical sectors such as health, housing and primary education did not receive the attention they deserved. India had a fairly sluggish rate of economic growth. In 1991, responding to a financial crisis and to the desire for higher rates of economic growth, India embarked on a programme of economic reforms that has sought increasingly to de-regulate various sectors including trade and foreign investment.

RESISTANCE TO GLOBALISATION

- Critics of globalisation make a variety of arguments. Those on the left argue that contemporary globalisation represents a particular phase of global capitalism that makes the rich richer (and fewer) and the poor poorer. Weakening of the state leads to a reduction in the capacity of the state to protect the interest of its poor. Critics of globalisation from the political right express anxiety over the political, economic and cultural effects. In political terms, they also fear the weakening of the state. Economically, they want a return to self-reliance and protectionism, at least in certain areas of the economy. Culturally, they are worried that traditional culture will be harmed and people will lose their age-old values and ways. Many anti- globalisation movements are not opposed to the idea of globalisation per se as much as they are opposed to a specific programme of globalisation, which they see as a form of imperialism. In 1999, at the World Trade Organisation (WTO) Ministerial Meeting there were widespread protests at Seattle alleging unfair trading practices by the economically powerful states. It was argued that the interests of the developing world were not given sufficient importance in the evolving global economic system. The World Social Forum (WSF) is another global platform, which brings together a wide coalition composed of human rights activists, environmentalists, labour, youth and women activists opposed to neo-liberal globalisation. The first WSF meeting was organised in Porto Alegre, Brazil in 2001. The fourth WSF meeting was held in Mumbai in 2004. The latest WSF meeting was held in Brazil in March 2018.

INDIA AND RESISTANCE TO GLOBALISATION

- Resistance to globalisation in India has come from different quarters. There have been left wing protests to economic liberalisation voiced through political parties as well as through forums like the Indian Social Forum. Trade unions of industrial workforce as well as those representing farmer interests have organised protests against the entry of multinationals. The patenting of certain plants like Neem by American and European firms has also generated considerable opposition.

25 Challenges of Nation Building

INTRODUCTION

- At the hour of midnight on 14-15 August 1947, India attained independence. Jawaharlal Nehru, the first prime minister of free India, addressed a special session of the Constituent Assembly that night. This was the famous 'tryst with destiny' speech.

- There were two goals almost everyone agreed upon: one, that after independence, we shall run our country through democratic government; and two, that the government will be run for the good of all, particularly the poor and the socially disadvantaged groups.

THREE CHALLENGES

- The first and the immediate challenge was to shape a nation that was united, yet accommodative of the diversity in our society. India was a land of continental size and diversity. Its people spoke different languages and followed different cultures and religions. The second challenge was to establish democracy. The Constitution granted fundamental rights and extended the right to vote to every citizen. India adopted representative democracy based on the parliamentary form of government. A democratic constitution is necessary but not sufficient for establishing a democracy. The challenge was to develop democratic practices in accordance with the Constitution. The third challenge was to ensure the development and wellbeing of the entire society and not only of some sections. Here again the Constitution clearly laid down the principle of equality and special protection to socially disadvantaged groups and religious and cultural communities. The Constitution also set out in the Directive Principles of State Policy the welfare goals that democratic politics must achieve. The real challenge now was to evolve effective policies for economic development and eradication of poverty.

- On 14-15 August 1947, not one but two nation- states came into existence. India and Pakistan. This was a result of 'partition', the division of British India into India and Pakistan. According to the 'two-nation theory' advanced by the Muslim League, India consisted of not one but two 'people', Hindus and Muslims. That is why it demanded Pakistan, a separate country for the Muslims. The Congress opposed this theory and the demand for Pakistan.

PROCESS OF PARTITION

- It was decided to follow the principle of religious majorities. This basically means that areas where the Muslims were in majority would make up the territory of Pakistan. There was no single belt of Muslim majority areas in British India. There were two areas of concentration, one in the west and one in the east. There was no way these two parts could be joined. So it was decided that the new country, Pakistan, will comprise two territories, West and East Pakistan separated by a long expanse of Indian Territory. Not all Muslim majority areas wanted to be in Pakistan. Khan Abdul Gaffar Khan, the undisputed leader of the North Western Frontier Province and known as 'Frontier Gandhi', was staunchly opposed to the two-nation theory. Eventually, his voice was simply ignored and the NWFP was made to merge with Pakistan. The third problem was that two of the Muslim majority provinces of British India, Punjab and Bengal, had very large areas where the non-Muslims were in majority. Eventually it was decided that these two provinces would be bifurcated according to the religious majority at the district or even lower level. This decision could not be made by the midnight of 14-15 August. It meant that a large number of people did not know on the day of Independence whether they were in India or in Pakistan. Fourth was the problem of 'minorities' on both sides of the border. Lakhs of Hindus and Sikhs in the areas that were now in Pakistan and an equally large number of Muslims on the Indian side of Punjab and Bengal (and to some extent Delhi and surrounding areas) found themselves trapped.

CONSEQUENCES OF PARTITION

- The year 1947 was the year of one of the largest, most abrupt, unplanned and tragic transfer of population that human history has known. There were killings and atrocities on both sides of the border. In the name of religion people of one community ruthlessly killed and maimed people of the other community. Cities like Lahore, Amritsar and Kolkata became divided into 'communal zones'. Muslims would avoid going into an area where mainly Hindus or Sikhs lived; similarly the Hindus and Sikhs stayed away from areas of Muslim predominance. Forced to abandon their homes and move across borders, people went through immense sufferings. Minorities on both sides of the border fled their home and often secured temporary shelter in 'refugee camps'. Even during this journey they were often attacked, killed or raped. Thousands of women were abducted on both sides of the border. They were made to convert to the religion of the abductor and were forced into marriage. In many cases women were killed by their own family members to preserve the 'family honour'. Many children were separated from their parents. It is estimated that the Partition forced about 80 lakh people to migrate across the new border. Between five to ten lakh people were killed in Partition related violence.

- On 30 January 1948, one such extremist, Nathuram Vinayak Godse, walked up to Gandhi ji during his evening prayer in Delhi and fired three bullets at him, killing him instantly. Thus ended a life long struggle for truth, non-violence, justice and tolerance.

THE PRINCELY STATES

- British India was divided into - the British Indian Provinces and the Princely States. The British Indian Provinces were directly under the control of the British government. On the other hand, several large and small states ruled by princes, called the Princely States, enjoyed some form of control over their internal affairs as long as they accepted British supremacy. This was called paramountcy or suzerainty of the British crown. Princely States covered one-third of the land area of the British Indian Empire and one out of four Indians lived under princely rule. Just before Independence it was announced by the British that with the end of their rule over India, paramountcy of the British crown over Princely States would also lapse. This meant that all these states, as many as 565 in all, would become legally independent. The British government took the view that all these states were free to join either India or Pakistan or remain independent if they so wished. This decision was left not to the people but to the princely rulers of these states. First of all, the ruler of Travancore announced that the state had decided on Independence. The Nizam of Hyderabad made a similar announcement the next day. Rulers like the Nawab of Bhopal were averse to joining the Constituent Assembly.

- The government's approach was guided by three considerations. Firstly, the people of most of the princely states clearly wanted to become part of the Indian union. Secondly, the government was prepared to be flexible in giving autonomy to some regions. The idea was to accommodate plurality and adopt a flexible approach in dealing with the demands of the regions. Thirdly, in the backdrop of Partition which brought into focus the contest over demarcation of territory, the integration and consolidation of the territorial boundaries of the nation had assumed supreme importance.

- Before15August1947,peaceful negotiations had brought almost all states whose territories were contiguous to the new boundaries of India, into the Indian Union. The rulers of most of the states signed a document called the 'Instrument of Accession' which meant that their state agreed to become a part of the Union of India. Accession of the Princely States of Junagadh, Hyderabad, Kashmir and Manipur proved more difficult than the rest. The issue of Junagarh was resolved after a plebiscite confirmed people's desire to join India.

Hyderabad

- Hyderabad, the largest of the Princely States was surrounded entirely by Indian Territory. Some parts of the old Hyderabad state are today parts of Maharashtra, Karnataka and Andhra Pradesh. Its ruler carried the title, 'Nizam', and he was one of the world's richest men. The Nizam wanted an independent status for Hyderabad. He entered into what was called the Standstill Agreement with India in November 1947 for a year while negotiations with the Indian government were going on. In the meantime, a movement of the people of Hyderabad State against the Nizam's rule gathered force. The peasantry in the Telangana region in particular, was the victim of Nizam's oppressive rule and rose against him. Women who had seen the worst of this oppression joined the movement in large numbers. Hyderabad town was the nerve centre of this movement. The Communists and the Hyderabad Congress were in the forefront of the movement. The Nizam responded by unleashing a para-military force known as the Razakars on the people. The atrocities and communal nature of the Razakars knew no bounds. They murdered, maimed, raped and looted, targeting particularly the non-Muslims. The central government had to order the army to tackle the situation. In September 1948, Indian army moved in to control the Nizam's forces. After a few days of intermittent fighting, the Nizam surrendered. This led to Hyderabad's accession to India.

Manipur

- A few days before Independence, the Maharaja of Manipur, Bodhachandra Singh, signed the Instrument of Accession with the Indian government on the assurance that the internal autonomy of Manipur would be maintained. Under the pressure of public opinion, the Maharaja held elections in Manipur in June 1948 and the state became a constitutional monarchy. Thus Manipur was the first part of India to hold an election based on universal adult franchise. In the Legislative Assembly of Manipur there were sharp differences over the question of merger of Manipur with India. While the state Congress wanted the merger, other political parties were opposed to this. The Government of India succeeded in pressurizing the Maharaja into signing a Merger Agreement in September 1949, without consulting the popularly elected Legislative Assembly of Manipur.

- During colonial rule, the state boundaries were drawn either on administrative convenience or simply coincided with the territories annexed by the British government or the territories ruled by the princely powers.

- Our national movement had rejected these divisions as artificial and had promised the linguistic principle as the basis of formation of states. In fact after the Nagpur session of Congress in 1920 the principle was recognised as the basis of the reorganisation of the Indian National Congress party itself. Many Provincial Congress Committees were created by linguistic zones, which did not follow the administrative divisions of British India.

Things changed after Independence and Partition

- Our leaders felt that carving out states on the basis of language might lead to disruption and disintegration. This decision of the national leadership was challenged by the local leaders and the people. Protests began in the Telugu speaking areas of the old Madras province, which included present day Tamil Nadu, parts of Andhra Pradesh, Kerala and Karnataka. The Vishalandhra movement (as the movement for a separate Andhra was called) demanded that the Telugu speaking areas should be separated from the Madras province of which they were a part and be made into a separate Andhra province. Nearly all the political forces in the Andhra region were in favour of linguistic reorganisation of the then Madras province. The movement gathered momentum as a result of the Central government's vacillation. Potti Sriramulu, a Congress leader and a veteran Gandhian, went on an indefinite fast that led to his death after 56 days. This caused great unrest and resulted in violent outbursts in Andhra region. People in large numbers took to the streets. Many were injured or lost their lives in police firing. In Madras, several legislators resigned their seats in protest. Finally, the Prime Minister announced the formation of a separate Andhra state in December 1952.

The formation of Andhra Pradesh

- It spurred the struggle for making of other states on linguistic lines in other parts of the country. These struggles forced the Central Government into appointing a States Reorganisation Commission in 1953 to look into the question of redrawing of the boundaries of states. The Commission in its report accepted that the boundaries of the state should reflect the boundaries of different languages. On the basis of its report the States Reorganisation Act was passed in 1956. This led to the creation of 14 states and six union territories.

- Above all, the linguistic states underlined the acceptance of the principle of diversity. When we say that India adopted democracy, it does not simply mean that India embraced a democratic constitution, nor does it merely mean that India adopted the format of elections. The choice was larger than that. It was a choice in favour of recognizing and accepting the existence of differences which could at times be oppositional. Democracy, in other words, was associated with plurality of ideas and ways of life.

- The states of Maharashtra and Gujarat were created in 1960.Statehood for Punjab came ten years later, in 1966, when the territories of today's Haryana and Himachal Pradesh were separated from the larger Punjab state. Meghalaya was carved out of Assam in 1972. Manipur and Tripura too emerged as separate states in the same year. The states of Mizoram and Arunachal Pradesh came into being in 1987. Nagaland had become a state much earlier in 1963. Three states Chhattisgarh, Uttarakhand and Jharkhand, were created in 2000.

26 Era of One-Party Dominance

CONGRESS DOMINANCE IN THE FIRST THREE GENERAL ELECTIONS

- The Congress party, as it was popularly known, had inherited the legacy of the national movement. It was the only party then to have an organization spread all over the country. And finally, in Jawaharlal Nehru, the party had the most popular and charismatic leader in Indian politics.
- The party won 364 of the 489 seats in the first Lok Sabha and finished way ahead of any other challenger. The Communist Party of India that came next in terms of seats won only 16 seats.

SOCIALIST PARTY

- The origins of the Socialist Party can be traced back to the mass movement stage of the Indian National Congress in the pre-independence era. In 1948, the Congress amended its constitution to prevent its members from having a dual party membership.
- The socialists believed in the ideology of democratic socialism which distinguished them both from the Congress as well as from the Communists.

CONGRESS AS SOCIAL AND IDEOLOGICAL COALITION

- The Congress began as a party dominated by the English speaking, upper caste, upper middle-class and urban elite. By the time of Independence, the Congress was transformed into a rainbow-like social coalition broadly representing India's diversity in terms of classes and castes, religions and languages and various interests.
- The Congress was a 'platform' for numerous groups, interests and even political parties to take part in the national movement.

EMERGENCE OF OPPOSITION PARTIES

- Opposition parties presence played a crucial role in maintaining the democratic character of the system. These parties offered a sustained and often principled criticism of the policies and practices of the Congress party.
- Jawaharlal Nehru often referred to his fondness for the Socialist Party and invited socialist leaders like Jayaprakash Narayan to join his government. This kind of personal relationship with and respect for political adversaries declined after the party competition grew more intense. Congress to accommodate all interests and all aspirants for political power steadily declined, other political parties started gaining greater significance.

27 Planning & Development

IDEAS OF DEVELOPMENT

- Development would mean different things for example, to an industrialist who is planning to set up a steel plant, to an urban consumer of steel and to the Adivasi who lives in that region.
- On the eve of Independence, India had before it, two models of modern development: the liberal-capitalist model as in much of Europe and the US and the socialist model as in the USSR.
- This reflected a broad consensus that had developed during the national movement. The nationalist leaders were clear that the economic concerns of the government of free India would have to be different from the narrowly defined commercial functions of the colonial government.

PLANNING

- In fact the idea of planning as a process of rebuilding economy earned a good deal of public support in the 1940s and 1950s all over the world.
- The Bombay Plan wanted the state to take major initiatives in industrial and other economic investments. Thus, from left to right, planning for development was the most obvious choice for the country after Independence.

The Early Initiative

- As in the USSR, the Planning Commission of India opted for five year plans (FYP). The idea is very simple: the Government of India prepares a document that has a plan for all its income and expenditure for the next five years. The First Five Year Plan:
- The First Five Year Plan (1951–1956) sought to get the country's economy out of the cycle of poverty. K.N. Raj, a young economist involved in drafting the plan, argued that India should 'hasten slowly' for the first two decades as a fast rate of development might endanger democracy. Agricultural sector was hit hardest by Partition and needed urgent attention. Huge allocations were made for large- scale projects like the Bhakhra Nangal Dam.

Rapid Industrialisation

- The Second FYP stressed on heavy industries. It was drafted by a team of economists and planners under the leadership of P. C. Mahalanobis. As savings and investment were growing in this period, a bulk of these industries like electricity, railways, steel, machineries and communication could be developed in the public sector. Indeed, such a push for industrialisation marked a turning point in India's development.

Agriculture versus industry

- Many thought that the Second Plan lacked an agrarian strategy for development, and the emphasis on industry caused agriculture and rural India to suffer. Others thought that without a drastic increase in industrial production, there could be no escape from the cycle of poverty. They argued that Indian planning did have an agrarian strategy to boost the production of food grains.

Public versus private sector

- India did not follow any of the two known paths to development – it did not accept the capitalist model of development in which development was left entirely to the private sector, nor did it follow the socialist model in which private property was abolished and all the production was controlled by the state. A mixed model like this was open to criticism from both the left and the right. Critics argued that the planners refused to provide the private sector with enough space and the stimulus to grow. The state intervened only in those areas where the private sector was not prepared to go. Thus the state helped the private sector to make profit.

LAND REFORMS

- Perhaps the most significant and successful of these was the abolition of the colonial system of zamindari. Attempts at consolidation of land – bringing small pieces of land together in one place so that the farm size could become viable for agriculture – were also fairly successful. It was not easy to turn these well-meaning policies on agriculture into genuine and effective action. This could happen only if the rural, landless poor were mobilised.

THE GREEN REVOLUTION

- The government adopted a new strategy for agriculture in order to ensure food sufficiency. Thus the government offered high-yielding variety seeds, fertilizers, pesticides and better irrigation at highly subsidised prices. The government also gave a guarantee to buy the produce of the farmers at a given price. The green revolution delivered only a moderate agricultural growth (mainly a rise in wheat production) and raised the availability of food in the country, but increased polarisation between classes and regions. Some regions like Punjab, Haryana and western Uttar Pradesh became agriculturally prosperous, while others remained backward.

28 India's External Relations

THE POLICY OF NON-ALIGNMENT

- The foreign policy of a nation reflects the interplay of domestic and external factors. Therefore, the noble ideals that inspired India's struggle for freedom influenced the making of its foreign policy.

Nehru's Role

- The first Prime Minister, Jawaharlal Nehru played a crucial role in setting the national agenda. He was the foreign minister himself . Thus both as the Prime Minister and the Foreign Minister, he exercised profound influence in the formulation and implementation of India's foreign policy from 1946 to 1964.

- The three major objectives of Nehru's foreign policy were to preserve the hard-earned sovereignty, protect territorial integrity, and promote rapid economic development.

Distance From Two Camps

- The foreign policy of independent India vigorously pursued the dream of a peaceful world by advocating the policy of non-alignment, by reducing Cold War tensions and by contributing human resources to the UN peacekeeping operations.

- India wanted to keep away from the military alliances led by US and Soviet Union against each other. While India was trying to convince the other developing countries about the policy of non-alignment, Pakistan joined the US-led military alliances.

Afro-Asian Unity

- Throughout the 1940s and 1950s, Nehru had been an ardent advocate of Asian unity. Under his leadership, India convened the Asian Relations Conference in March 1947, five months ahead of attaining its independence. The Afro Asian conference held in the Indonesian city of Bandung in 1955, commonly known as the Bandung Conference, marked the zenith of India's engagement with the newly independent Asian and African nations. The Bandung Conference later led to the establishment of the NAM. The First Summit of the NAM was held in Belgrade in September 1961. Nehru was a co-founder of the NAM.

PEACE AND CONFLICT WITH CHINA

- Unlike its relationship with Pakistan, free India began its relationship with China on a very friendly note. After the Chinese revolution in 1949, India was one of the first countries to recognise the communist government.

The Chinese Invasion, 1962

- The Tibetan spiritual leader, the Dalai Lama, sought and obtained political asylum in India in 1959. China alleged that the government of India was allowing anti-China activities to take place from within India.

- China claimed two areas within the Indian territory: Aksai- chin area in the Ladakh region of Jammu and Kashmir and much of the state of Arunachal Pradesh in what was then called NEFA (North Eastern Frontier Agency). China launched a swift and massive invasion in October 1962 on both the disputed regions.

- The China war dented India's image at home and abroad. India had to approach the Americans and the British for military assistance to tide over the crisis. The Soviet Union remained neutral during the conflict. It induced a sense of national humiliation and at the same time strengthened a spirit of nationalism. The party split in 1964 and the leaders of the latter faction formed the Communist Party of India (Marxist) (CPI-M).

- The process of its reorganization began soon after the China war. Nagaland was granted statehood; Manipur and Tripura, though Union Territories were given the right to elect their own legislative assemblies.

WARS AND PEACE WITH PAKISTAN

- The Kashmir conflict did not prevent cooperation between the governments of India and Pakistan. Both the governments worked together to restore the women abducted during Partition to their original families. The India Pakistan Indus Waters Treaty was signed by Nehru and General Ayub Khan in 1960.

- A more serious armed conflict between the two countries began in 1965. As you would read in the next chapter, by then Lal Bahadur Shastri had taken over as the Prime Minister. In April 1965 Pakistan launched armed attacks in the Rann of Kutch area of Gujarat.

- The hostilities came to an end with the UN intervention. Later, Indian Prime Minister Lal Bahadur Shastri and Pakistan's General Ayub Khan signed the Tashkent Agreement, brokered by the Soviet Union, in January 1966.

BANGLADESH WAR, 1971

- Beginning in 1970, Pakistan faced its biggest internal crisis. The country's first general election produced a split verdict – Zulfikar Ali Bhutto's party emerged a winner in West Pakistan, while the Awami League led by Sheikh Mujib-ur Rahman swept through East Pakistan.

- Instead, in early 1971, the Pakistani army arrested Sheikh Mujib and unleashed a reign of terror on the people of East Pakistan.

- In response to this, the people started a struggle to liberate 'Bangladesh' from Pakistan. Throughout 1971, India had to bear the burden of about 80 lakh refugees who fled East Pakistan and took shelter in the neighbouring areas in India. India extended moral and material support to the freedom struggle in Bangladesh. Pakistan accused India of a conspiracy to break it up.

- Support for Pakistan came from the US and China. In order to counter the US-Pakistan-China axis, India signed a 20-year Treaty of Peace and Friendship with the Soviet Union in August 1971. This treaty assured India of Soviet support if the country faced any attack. After months of diplomatic tension and military build-up, a full-scale war between India and Pakistan broke out in December 1971. Welcomed and supported by the local population, the Indian army made rapid progress in East Pakistan. Within ten days the Indian army had surrounded Dhaka from three sides and the Pakistani army of about 90,000 had to surrender. With Bangladesh as a free country, India declared a unilateral ceasefire. Later, the signing of the Shimla Agreement between Indira Gandhi and Zulfikar Ali Bhutto on 3 July 1972 formalized the return of peace. India, with its limited resources, had initiated development planning. However, conflicts with neighbours derailed the five-year plans. The scarce resources were diverted to the defence sector especially after 1962, as India had to embark on a military modernisation drive.

INDIA'S NUCLEAR POLICY

- Another crucial development of this period was the first nuclear explosion undertaken by India in May 1974. Nehru had always put his faith in science and technology for rapidly building a modern India. A significant component of his industrialisation plans was the nuclear programme initiated in the late 1940s under the guidance of Homi J. Bhabha.

- When Communist China conducted nuclear tests in October 1964, the five nuclear weapon powers, the US, USSR, UK, France, and China (Taiwan then represented China) – also the five Permanent Members of the UN Security Council – tried to impose the Nuclear Non-proliferation Treaty (NPT) of 1968 on the rest of the world. India always considered the NPT as discriminatory and had refused to sign it.

- When India conducted its first nuclear test, it was termed as peaceful explosion. India argued that it was committed to the policy of using nuclear power only for peaceful purposes.

- The period when the nuclear test was conducted was a difficult period in domestic politics. Following the Arab- Israel War of 1973, the entire world was affected by the Oil Shock due to the massive hike in the oil prices by the Arab nations. It led to economic turmoil in India resulting in high inflation.

29

The Challenges to Democracy

BANGLADESH WAR AND ECONOMIC CRISIS

- The Bangladesh crisis had put a heavy strain on India's economy. About eight million people crossed over the East Pakistan border into India. This was followed by war with Pakistan. After the war the U.S government stopped all aid to India. In the international market, oil prices increased manifold during this period. Prices increased by 23 per cent in 1973 and 30 per cent in 1974. Such a high level of inflation caused much hardship to the people.

- Monsoons failed in 1972-1973. This resulted in a sharp decline in agricultural productivity. Food grain output declined by 8 per cent. There was also an increase in the activities of Marxist groups who did not believe in parliamentary politics. These groups had taken to arms and insurgent techniques for the overthrow of the capitalist order and the established political system.

GUJARAT AND BIHAR MOVEMENTS

- In January 1974 students in Gujarat started an agitation against rising prices of food grains, cooking oil and other essential commodities, and against corruption in high places. Under intense pressure from students, supported by the opposition political parties, assembly elections were held in Gujarat in June 1975. Jayaprakash Narayan demanded the dismissal of the Congress government in Bihar and gave a call for total revolution in the social, economic and political spheres in order to establish what he considered to be true democracy.

- Jayaprakash Narayan wanted to spread the Bihar movement to other parts of the country. Alongside the agitation led by Jayaprakash Narayan, the employees of the Railways gave a call for a nationwide strike.

CONFLICT WITH JUDICIARY

- This was also the period when the government and the ruling party had many differences with the judiciary. Two developments further added to the tension between the judiciary and the executive. Immediately after the Supreme Court's decision in 1973 in the Kesavananda Bharati case, a vacancy arose for the post of the Chief Justice of India.

DECLARATION OF EMERGENCY

- This order came on an election petition filed by Raj Narain, a socialist leader and a candidate who had contested against her in 1971. The petition, challenged the election of Indira Gandhi on the ground that she had used the services of government servants in her election campaign.

Crisis And Response

- The opposition political parties led by Jayaprakash Narayan pressed for Indira Gandhi's resignation and organised a massive demonstration in Delhi's Ramlila grounds on 25 June 1975. Jayaprakash announced a nationwide satyagraha for her resignation and asked the army, the police and government employees not to obey "illegal and immoral orders".

- The response of the government was to declare a state of emergency. On 25 June 1975, the government declared that there was a threat of internal disturbances and therefore, it invoked Article 352 of the Constitution.

- Once an emergency is proclaimed, the federal distribution of powers remains practically suspended and all the powers are concentrated in the hands of the union government.

- On the night of 25 June 1975, the Prime Minister recommended the imposition of Emergency to President Fakhruddin Ali Ahmed. He issued the proclamation immediately. After midnight, the electricity to all the major newspaper offices was disconnected.

Consequences

- Deciding to use its special powers under Emergency provisions, the government suspended the freedom of the Press. Newspapers were asked to get prior approval for all material to be published. This is known as press censorship. Several High Courts gave judgments that even after the declaration of Emergency the courts could entertain a writ of habeas corpus filed by a person challenging his/her detention.

- Many journalists were arrested for writing against the Emergency. The forty-second amendment was also passed during the Emergency. Among the various changes made by this amendment, one was that the duration of the legislatures in the country was extended from five to six years. Besides this, during an Emergency, elections can be postponed by one year.

- The 1977 elections turned into a referendum on the experience of the Emergency, at least in north India where the impact of the Emergency was felt most strongly. The lesson was clear and has been reiterated in many state level elections thereafter – governments that are perceived to be anti-democratic are severely punished by the voters.

LESSONS OF THE EMERGENCY

- The Emergency at once brought out both the weaknesses and the strengths of India's democracy. Emergency made everyone more aware of the value of civil liberties. The Courts too, have taken an active role after the Emergency in protecting the civil liberties of the individuals. the actual implementation of the Emergency rule took place through the police and the administration. These institutions could not function independently.

POLITICS AFTER EMERGENCY

- The 1977 elections turned into a referendum on the experience of the Emergency, at least in north India where the impact of the Emergency was felt most strongly. The lesson was clear and has been reiterated in many state level elections thereafter – governments that are perceived to be anti-democratic are severely punished by the voters.

Lok Sabha Elections, 1977

- Accordingly, all the leaders and activists were released from jails. Elections were held in March 1977. This left the opposition with very little time, but political developments took place very rapidly. The Janata Party made this election into a referendum on the Emergency. Its campaign was focused on the non- democratic character of the rule and on the various excesses that took place during this period.

JANATA GOVERNMENT

- The Janata Party government that came to power after the 1977 elections was far from cohesive. The opposition to Emergency could keep the Janata Party together only for a while. Its critics felt that the Janata Party lacked direction, leadership, and a common programme. The Janata Party split and the government which was led by Morarji Desai lost its majority in less than 18 months. Another government headed by Charan Singh was formed on the assurance of the support of the Congress party.

Rise of Popular Movements

CHIPKO MOVEMENT

- Location- Uttarakhand in early 1973
- Villagers protested against the practices of commercial logging that the government had permitted.
- They used a novel tactic for their protest – that of hugging the trees to prevent them from being cut down.
- The struggle soon spread across many parts of the Uttarakhand region.
- Larger issues of ecological and economic exploitation of the region were raised.
- The villagers demanded that no forest-exploiting contracts should be given to outsiders and local communities should have effective control over natural resources like land, water and forests.
- The movement took up economic issues of landless forest workers and asked for guarantees of minimum wage.
- Women's active participation in the Chipko agitation was a very novel aspect of the movement.
- The movement achieved a victory when the government issued a ban on felling of trees in the Himalayan regions for fifteen years
- The Chipko movement, which started over a single issue, became a symbol of many such popular movements emerging in different parts of the country during the 1970s and later.

DALIT PANTHERS

- Dalit Panthers, a militant organisation of the Dalit youth, was formed in Maharashtra in 1972
- In the post-Independence period, Dalit groups were mainly fighting against the perpetual caste based inequalities and material injustices
- Effective implementation of reservations and other such policies of social justice was one of their prominent demands.
- The Dalit Panthers resorted to mass action for assertion of Dalits' rights.

- As a result of sustained agitations, the government passed a comprehensive law in 1989 that provided rigorous punishment for doing atrocities on Dalits

- The movement provided a platform for Dalit educated youth to use their creativity as a protest activity.

- In the post- Emergency period, Dalit Panthers got involved in electoral compromises which led to its decline.

- Organisations like the Backward and Minority Communities' Employees Federation (BAMCEF) took over this space.

BHARATIYA KISAN UNION

- Meerut agitation - January 1988

- Around twenty thousand farmers had gathered in the city of Meerut, Uttar Pradesh.

- They were protesting against the government decision to increase electricity rates.

- The farmers camped for about three weeks outside the district collector's office until their demands were fulfilled.

- The Meerut agitation was seen as a great show of rural power – power of farmer cultivators.

- These agitating farmers were members of the Bharatiya Kisan Union (BKU), an organisation of farmers from western Uttar Pradesh and Haryana regions.

- The BKU was one of the leading organisations in the farmers' movement of the eighties.

- Most of the BKU members belonged to a single community.

- The organisation used traditional caste panchayats of these communities in bringing them together over economic issues.

- The BKU distanced itself from all political parties. It operated as a pressure group in politics with its strength of sheer numbers.

- Like the BKU, farmers' organisations across States recruited their members from communities that dominated regional electoral politics.

- Shetkari Sanghatana of Maharashtra and Rayata Sangha of Karnataka, are prominent examples of such organisations of the farmers.

ANTI-ARRACK MOVEMENT

- When the BKU was mobilising the farmers of the north, an altogether different kind of mobilisation in the rural areas was taking shape in the southern State of Andhra Pradesh.

- It was a spontaneous mobilisation of women demanding a ban on the sale of alcohol in their neighbourhoods.

- Rural women in remote villages from the State of Andhra Pradesh fought a battle against alcoholism, against mafias and against the government during this period (1992).

- These agitations shaped what was known as the anti-arrack movement in the State.

Linkages

- Gradually this anti-arrack movement touched upon larger social, economic and political issues of the region that affected women's life.

- Groups of local women tried to address these complex issues in their agitation against arrack. They also openly discussed the issue of domestic violence.

- Their movement, for the first time, provided a platform to discuss private issues of domestic violence. Thus, the anti-arrack movement also became part of the women's movement.

- As a result the movement made demands of equal representation to women in politics during the nineties. (73rd and 74th amendments have granted reservations to women in local level political offices.)

NARMADA BACHAO AANDOLAN

- An ambitious developmental project was launched in the Narmada valley of central India in early eighties.

- The project consisted of 30 big dams, 135 medium sized and around 3,000 small dams to be constructed on the Narmada and its tributaries that flow across three states of Madhya Pradesh, Gujarat and Maharashtra.

- Sardar Sarovar Project in Gujarat and the Narmada Sagar Project in Madhya Pradesh were two of the most important and biggest, multi- purpose dams planned under the project.

- Narmada Bachao Aandolan, a movement to save Narmada , opposed the construction of these dams.

Sardar Sarovar Project

- It is a multipurpose mega-scale dam.

- In the process of construction of the dam 245 villages from these States were expected to get submerged.

- It required relocation of around two and a half lakh people from these villages.

- Issues of relocation and proper rehabilitation of the project-affected people were first raised by local activist groups.

- It was around 1988-89 that the issues crystallised under the banner of the NBA – a loose collective of local voluntary organisations.

Demands raised by the voluntary organisations

- The movement demanded proper and just rehabilitation of all those who were directly or indirectly affected by the project.

- The movement also questioned the nature of decision-making processes that go in the making of mega scale developmental projects.

- The NBA insisted that local communities must have a say in such decisions and they should also have effective control over natural resources like water, land and forests.

Achievement of the movement

- Right to rehabilitation has been now recognised by the government and the judiciary.
- A comprehensive National Rehabilitation Policy formed by the government in 2003.

Construction of the dam

- The Supreme Court upheld the government's decision to go ahead with the construction of the dam while also instructing to ensure proper rehabilitation.

The course of NBA

- Narmada Bachao Aandolan continued a sustained agitation for more than twenty years.
- It used every available democratic strategy to put forward its demands.
- However, the movement could not garner much support among the mainstream political parties – including the opposition parties.
- By the end of the 'nineties, however, the NBA was not alone.
- There emerged many local groups and movements that challenged the logic of large scale developmental projects in their areas.

MOVEMENT FOR RIGHT TO INFORMATION

- The movement started in 1990, when a mass based organisation called the Mazdoor Kisan Shakti Sangathan (MKSS) in Rajasthan took the initiative in demanding records of famine relief work and accounts of labourers.
- In 1996 MKSS formed National Council for People's Right to Information in Delhi to raise RTI to the status of a national campaign.
- Prior to that, the Consumer Education and Research Center, the Press Council and the Shourie committee had proposed a draft RTI law.
- In 2002, a weak Freedom of Information Act was legislated but never came into force.
- In 2004 RTI Bill was tabled and received presidential assent in June 2005

CHAPTER 31

Regional Aspirations

INTRODUCTION

- Indian approach to diversity – the Indian nation shall not deny the rights of different regions and linguistic groups to retain their own culture.

- Indian nationalism sought to balance the principles of unity and diversity.

- The Indian approach was very different from the one adopted in many European countries where they saw cultural diversity as a threat to the nation.

- India adopted a democratic approach to the question of diversity.

- Democracy allows the political expressions of regional aspirations

- Democratic politics allows parties and groups to address the people on the basis of their regional identity, aspiration and specific regional problems.

- Such an arrangement may sometimes lead to tensions and problems.

- Sometimes, the concern for national unity may overshadow the regional needs and aspirations.

- At other times a concern for region alone may blind us to the larger needs of the nation.

AREAS OF TENSION

- The issue of Jammu and Kashmir - It was a question of the political aspirations of the people of Kashmir valley.

- In some parts of the north-east, there was no consensus about being a part of India (eg. Nagaland and Mizoram)

- In the south, some groups from the Dravid movement briefly toyed with the idea of a separate country.

- Today's Andhra Pradesh, Karnataka, Maharashtra, and Gujarat were among the regions affected by mass agitations.

- There were protests against making Hindi the official national language of the country(in Tamil Nadu)

- In the north, there were strong pro-Hindi agitations demanding that Hindi be made the official language

- From the late 1950s, people speaking the Punjabi language started agitating for a separate State for themselves.
- This demand was finally accepted and the States of Punjab and Haryana were created in 1966.
- Later, the States of Chhattisgarh, Uttarakhand and Jharkhand were created.
- Thus the challenge of diversity was met by redrawing the internal boundaries of the country.

JAMMU AND KASHMIR

- Jammu and Kashmir had a special status under Article 370 of the Indian Constitution.
- Jammu and Kashmir comprises three social and political regions— Jammu, Kashmir and Ladakh.
- The Jammu region is a mix of foothills and plains.
- It is predominantly inhabited by the Hindus.
- The Kashmir region mainly comprises of the Kashmir valley.
- It is inhabited mostly by Kashmiri Muslims with the remaining being Hindus, Sikhs, Buddhists and others.
- The Ladakh region is mainly mountainous. It has very little population which is almost equally divided between Buddhists and Muslims.

Roots of the Problem

- Before 1947, Jammu and Kashmir (J&K) was a Princely State under the rule of. Maharaja Hari Singh
- The ruler of Kashmir, Maharaja Hari Singh did not want to merge either with India or Pakistan but to have an independent status for his state.
- In October 1947, Pakistan sent tribal infiltrators from its side to capture Kashmir.
- This forced the Maharaja to ask for Indian military help.
- India extended the military support and drove back the infiltrators from Kashmir valley, but only after the Maharaja had signed an 'Instrument of Accession' with the Government of India.
- The issue was taken to the Union Nations Organisation, which in its resolution dated 21 April 1948 recommended a three step process to resolve the issue.
- Firstly, Pakistan had to withdraw its entire nationalities, who entered into Kashmir.
- Secondly, India needed to progressively reduce its forces so as to maintain law and order. Thirdly, a plebiscite was to be conducted in a free and impartial manner.
- However, no progress could be achieved under this resolution.

Politics since 1948 (Politics in India since Independence)

- Sheikh Abdullah took over as the Prime Minister of the State of J&K in March 1948 while India agreed to grant it provisional autonomy under the Article 370.
- The head of the government in the State was then called Prime Minister.
- He was dismissed in 1953 by the Centre government and kept in detention for a number of years.

- A change in the provision of the Constitution of Jammu and Kashmir was made in 1965 by which the Prime Minister of the state was designated as Chief Minister of the state.
- Accordingly, Ghulam Mohammed Sadiq of the Indian National Congress became the first Chief Minister of the state.
- In 1974 Sheikh Abdullah became the Chief Minister of the State.
- Sheikh Abdullah died in 1982 and the leadership of the National Conference went to his son, Farooq Abdullah, who became the Chief Minister.

Insurgency and After

- By 1989, the State had come in the grip of a militant movement mobilised around the cause of a separate Kashmiri nation.
- The insurgents got moral, material and military support from Pakistan.
- For a number of years the State was under President's rule and effectively under the control of the armed forces.
- Throughout the period from 1990, Jammu and Kashmir experienced extraordinary violence at the hands of the insurgents and through army action.
- Assembly elections were held in 1996 in which the National Conference led by Farooq Abdullah came to power with a demand for regional autonomy for Jammu and Kashmir.
- At the end of its term, elections were held in the State in 2002.
- The National Conference failed to win a majority and was replaced by a coalition government of People's Democratic Party (PDP) and Congress.

2002 and Beyond

- President rule was imposed in the state in July 2008.
- The next election was held in November- December 2008.
- Another coalition government (composed of NC and INC) came into power headed by Omar Abdullah in 2009.
- In 2014, the state went into another election, which recorded the highest voters' turnout in 25 years.
- A coalition government led by Mufti Mohammed Sayeed of the PDP came into power with the BJP as its partner.
- After Mufti Mohammed Sayeed died, his daughter Mahbooba Mufti became the first woman Chief Minister of the state in April 2016.
- The President's rule was imposed in June 2018 after BJP withdrew its support to the Mufti government.
- On 5 August 2019, Article 370 was abolished by the Jammu & Kashmir Reorganisation Act 2019 and the state was constituted into two Union Territories, viz., Jammu & Kashmir and Ladakh.

PUNJAB

- The decade of 1980s also witnessed major developments in the State of Punjab.
- The social composition of the State changed first with Partition and later on after the carving out of Haryana and Himachal Pradesh.

- While the rest of the country was reorganised on linguistic lines in 1950s, Punjab had to wait till 1966 for the creation of a Punjabi speaking State.
- The Akali Dal, which was formed in 1920 as the political wing of the Sikhs, had led the movement for the formation of a 'Punjabi suba'.

Political context

- After the reorganisation, the Akalis came to power in 1967 and then in 1977.
- On both the occasions it was a coalition government.
- During the 1970s a section of Akalis began to demand political autonomy for the region.
- The Anandpur Sahib Resolution(1973) passed by the Akalis asserted regional autonomy and wanted to redefine centre-state relationship in the country.
- The Resolution was a plea for strengthening federalism, but it could also be interpreted as a plea for a separate Sikh nation.
- The Akali government got dismissed in 1980
- After that , the Akali Dal launched a movement on the question of the distribution of water between Punjab and its neighbouring States.

Cycle of violence

- Soon, the leadership of the movement passed from the moderate Akalis to the extremist elements and took the form of armed insurgency.
- These militants made their headquarters inside the Sikh holy shrine, the Golden Temple in Amritsar, and turned it into an armed fortress.
- In June 1984, the Government of India carried out 'Operation Blue Star', code name for army action in the Golden Temple.
- In this operation, the Government could successfully flush out the militants, but it also damaged the historic temple and deeply hurt the sentiments of the Sikhs.
- This military operation gave further impetus to militant and extremist groups.
- Prime Minister Indira Gandhi was assassinated on 31 October 1984 outside her residence by her bodyguards.
- Both the assassins were Sikhs and wanted to take revenge for Operation Bluestar.
- In Delhi and in many parts of northern India violence broke out against the Sikh community. The violence against the Sikhs continued for almost a week.

Road to Peace

- In 1984, the new Prime Minister Rajiv Gandhi initiated a dialogue with moderate Akali leaders.
- In July 1985, he reached an agreement with Harchand Singh Longowal, then the President of the Akali Dal.
- This agreement, known as the Rajiv Gandhi - Longowal Accord or the Punjab Accord, was a step towards bringing normalcy to Punjab.
- It was agreed that Chandigarh would be transferred to Punjab, a separate commission would be appointed to resolve the border dispute between Punjab and Haryana, and a tribunal would be set up to decide the sharing of Ravi-Beas river water among Punjab, Haryana and Rajasthan.

- The agreement also provided for compensation to and better treatment of those affected by the militancy in Punjab and the withdrawal of the application of Armed Forces Special Powers Act in Punjab.
- However, peace did not come easily or immediately. The cycle of violence continued nearly for a decade.
- Militancy was eventually eradicated by the security forces. But the losses incurred by the people of Punjab – Sikhs and Hindus alike – were enormous.
- Peace returned to Punjab by the middle of 1990s
- The alliance of Akali Dal (Badal) and the BJP scored a major victory in1997, in the first normal elections in the State in the post-militancy era.

NORTH-EAST

- In the North-East, regional aspirations reached a turning point in 1980s.
- This region now consists of seven States, also referred to as the 'seven sisters'.
- The region has only 4 per cent of the country's population but about twice as much share of its area.
- A small corridor of about 22 kilometres connects the region to the rest of the country. Otherwise the region shares boundaries with China, Myanmar and Bangladesh and serves as India's gateway to South East Asia.
- Tripura, Manipur and Khasi Hills of Meghalaya were erstwhile Princely States which merged with India after Independence.
- Nagaland State was created in 1963; Manipur, Tripura and Meghalaya in 1972 while Mizoram and Arunachal Pradesh became separate States only in 1987.
- The Partition of India in 1947 had reduced the North-East to a land locked region and affected its economy.
- Cut off from the rest of India, the region suffered neglect in developmental terms.
- The vast international border and weak communication between the North-East and the rest of India have further added to the delicate nature of politics there.
- Three issues dominate the politics of North-East: demands for autonomy, movements for secession, and opposition to 'outsiders'.
- Major initiatives on the first issue in the 1970s set the stage for some dramatic developments on the second and the third in the 1980s.

Demands for autonomy

- At independence the entire region except Manipur and Tripura comprised the State of Assam.
- Demands for political autonomy arose when the non-Assamese felt that the Assam government
- The Central Government had to create Meghalaya, Mizoram and Arunachal Pradesh out of Assam.
- Tripura and Manipur were upgraded into States too.
- The reorganisation of the North-East was completed by 1972.

- But this was not the end of autonomy demands in this region.
- In Assam, for example, communities like the Bodos, Karbis and Dimasas wanted separate States.
- Karbis and Dimasas have been granted autonomy under District Councils while Bodos were recently granted Autonomous Council.

Secessionist movements (Mizoram and Nagaland)

- After Independence, the Mizo Hills area was made an autonomous district within Assam.
- Some Mizos believed that they were never a part of British India and therefore did not belong to the Indian union.
- But the movement for secession gained popular support after the Assam government failed to respond adequately to the great famine of 1959 in Mizo hills.
- The Mizos' anger led to the formation of the Mizo National Front (MNF) under the leadership of Laldenga.
- In 1966 the MNF started an armed campaign for independence.
- Thus, started a two decade long battle between Mizo insurgents and the Indian army.
- The MNF fought a guerrilla war, got support from Pakistani government and secured shelter in the then East Pakistan.
- The Indian security forces countered it with a series of repressive measures
- At the end of two decades of insurgency everyone was a loser.
- Laldenga came back from exile in Pakistan and started negotiations with the Indian government.
- Rajiv Gandhi steered these negotiations to a positive conclusion.
- In 1986 a peace agreement was signed between Rajiv Gandhi and Laldenga.
- As per this accord Mizoram was granted full- fledged statehood with special powers and the MNF agreed to give up secessionist struggle. Laldenga took over as the Chief Minister.
- The story of Nagaland is similar to Mizoram, except that it started much earlier and has not yet had such a happy ending.
- Led by Angami Zaphu Phizo, a section of the Nagas declared independence from India way back in 1951. Phizo turned down many offers of negotiated settlement. The Naga National Council launched an armed struggle for sovereignty of Nagas.
- After a period of violent insurgency a section of the Nagas signed an agreement with the Government of India but this was not acceptable to other rebels. The problem in Nagaland still awaits a final resolution.

Movements against outsiders

- The Assam Movement from 1979 to 1985 is the best example of movements against 'outsiders'. The Assamese suspected that there were huge numbers of illegal Bengali Muslim settlers from Bangladesh.
- They felt that unless these foreign nationals are detected and deported they would reduce the indigenous Assamese into a minority.

- In 1979 the All Assam Students' Union (AASU), a students' group not affiliated to any party, led an anti-foreigner movement.
- The movement was against illegal migrations, against domination of Bengalis and other outsiders, and against faulty voters' register that included the names of lakhs of immigrants.
- The movement demanded that all outsiders who had entered the State after 1951 should be sent back.
- Eventually after six years of turmoil, the Rajiv Gandhi-led government entered into negotiations with the AASU leaders, leading to the signing of an accord in 1985.
- According to this agreement those foreigners who migrated into Assam during and after Bangladesh war and since, were to be identified and deported.
- Assam accord brought peace and changed the face of politics in Assam, but it did not solve the problem of immigration.
- The issue of the 'outsiders' continues to be a live issue in the politics of Assam and many other places in the North-East.

GOA'S LIBERATION

- Although the British empire in India came to an end in 1947, Portugal refused to withdraw from the territories of Goa, Diu and Daman which were under its colonial rule since the sixteenth century.
- During their long rule, the Portuguese suppressed the people of Goa, denied them civil rights, and carried out forced religious conversions.
- After India's Independence, the Indian government tried very patiently to persuade the Portuguese government to withdraw.
- Finally, in December 1961, the Government of India sent the army which liberated these territories after barely two days of action. Goa, Diu and Daman became Union Territory.
- In January 1967, the Central Government held a special 'opinion poll' in Goa asking people to decide if they wanted to be part of Maharashtra or remain separate.
- A referendum-like procedure was used to ascertain people's wishes on this issue.
- The majority voted in favour of remaining outside of Maharashtra.
- Thus, Goa continued as a Union Territory.
- Finally, in 1987, Goa became a State of the Indian Union.

32 Post Independence Developments Till Present

CHRONOLOGY OF MAJOR POST-INDEPENDENCE EVENTS

India gains Independence (1947)

- India wins independence from Britain after being divided into two separate nations, India and Pakistan. Jawaharlal Nehru is appointed the first prime minister.

Partition (1947)

- British India was divided into two countries India and Pakistan along sectarian lines.
- British judge Cyril Radcliffe took a mere 40 days to draw 6,100 km of new boundaries both to India's west and east.
- This resulted in unprecedented scenes as a million people were killed (some estimates put the toll at double this) and 15 million migrated to either side of the border, on foot or on trains.

The first Kashmir War (1947-1948)

- It was fought between India and Pakistan over the princely state of Jammu and Kashmir from 1947 to 1948. It ended with Maharaja Hari Singh signing an Instrument of Accession to India.
- October 26, Maharaja Hari Singh of Jammu and Kashmir, signed the instrument of accession to India.
- Instrument of accession – It became central to Article 370, abrogated by the BJP in 2019.
- In 1948, Prime Minister Nehru took the matter to the United Nations, which passed a resolution calling for a ceasefire, the withdrawal of Pakistani troops and tribal militia, and finally a referendum. But the armies never pulled back, giving rise to today's Pakistan Occupied Kashmir, and the referendum never took place, giving rise to an angst that Pakistan based terror groups exploit.

Mahatma Gandhi is assassinated (1948)

- On January 30, 1948, Mahatma Gandhi was assassinated by Nathuram Godse

India becomes a republic as its constitution comes into effect (1950)

- India came into its own as a democratic republic on January 26, 1950 – a day celebrated since as Republic Day.
- The Constitution was written by India's finest minds, led by BR Ambedkar, with the Constituent Assembly sitting for 11 sessions, and 167 days over 2 years and 11 months.
- The Constitution set the framework for India's politics, adopting Universal Adult Franchise – the inalienable right of all citizens to vote and to participate in India's democratic process.

Railways Nationalisation (1951)

- Railways network was nationalised in 1951 and was initially divided into three zones.
- Indian Railways is now one of the world's largest railway networks comprising 119,630 km of tracks and 7,216 stations.

First general elections (1951)

- India took a democratic leap by conducting its first general elections in 1951, with Congress registering a thumping victory by winning 364 of the 489 seats. Jawaharlal Nehru became India's first prime minister.

First Asian Games (1951)

- India hosted the first-ever Asian Games in the year 1951 in New Delhi.

The first IIT comes up in Kharagpur (1951)

- In July 1951, India set up the first Indian Institute of Technology (IIT) in Kharagpur, in what was envisaged as a world quality engineering school that would create technicians to, quite literally, build the nation.
- India's first election was led by first election commissioner Sukumar Sen

Bharatiya Jana Sangh (1951)

- One of the parties that contested the first general election was the Bharatiya Jana Sangh, founded in October 1951.
- The Sangh was the precursor to the Bharatiya Janata Party, and led by Shyama Prasad Mukherjee, who had served in Nehru's interim cabinet.

Bhoodan Movement (1951)

- The Bhoodan Movement was initiated by Acharya Vinoba Bhave in 1951, based on the principle of voluntary land redistribution.
- Vinoba Bhave started the Sarvodya Samaj, a federation of constructive workers.
- Vinoba Bhave, along with his supporters, undertook a foot march or padyatra to encourage landowners to donate at least 1/6th of their land to landless people.

Panchsheel Agreement (1954)

- The Panchsheel Agreement was a five-point agreement between India and China, signed on 29 April 1954.

- The agreement consisted of five principles which were to govern their relations: mutual recognition of one another's sovereignty and territorial integrity, Non-aggression pact, mutual non-interference with each other's domestic affairs, equality as well as mutual benefit, as well as coexistence in peace

States Reorganisation Act (1955)

- In 1953, the government was forced to separate Andhra Pradesh (from Madras state) for Telugu speakers.
- In the aftermath, as more such demands rose, the government appointed a commission, which suggested in 1955 that the country be divided into 16 states and three union territories on the basis of language.
- Eventually, the government moved to create 14 states and 6 Union Territories through the States Reorganisation Act, 1956 - This remains the largest reorganisation of states.
- Punjab and Haryana were separated on linguistic lines a decade later, but other more recent divisions – such as Uttarakhand from Uttar Pradesh, Jharkhand from Bihar, and Chhattisgarh from Madhya Pradesh in the year 2000, have been based on administrative and social considerations rather than linguistic ones.

Asia's first nuclear reactor (1956)

- India designed and built Asia's first nuclear reactor Apsara nuclear reactor on August 4, 1956.

Mother India (1957)

- *Mother India* (directed by Mehboob Khan) was the first Indian movie to be nominated for the Best Foreign Language Film Oscar.

Dalai Lama seeks asylum (1959)

- India played a significant role in the conflict and gave refuge to the Dalai Lama who set up a government in exile in Dharamshala
- The 1959 crisis in Tibet saw a revolt erupt in Lhasa, its capital, which had been virtually under Chinese control after the Seventeen Point Agreement in 1951.

Green Revolution (1960)

- The Green Revolution was a period that began in the 1960s during which agriculture in India was converted into a modern industrial system by the adoption of technology, such as the use of high yielding variety seeds, mechanised farm tools, irrigation facilities, pesticides and fertilizers.
- The Green Revolution in India in 1960 saw an increase in food grain production, with development of high-yielding varieties of wheat and pulses.

First Non Aligned Summit is held (1961)

- Non Aligned Movement (NAM) is an international forum of 120 developing countries that believe in the idea of non-alignment with the major power blocs (USA and USSR)

- It was established in 1961 in Belgrade, former Yugoslavia under the leadership of the then Indian Prime Minister Pandit Jawaharlal Nehru, President of Egypt Gamal Abdel Nasser and the President of Yugoslavia Josip Broz Tito.
- In 1961, the first conference of heads of state or government of non-aligned countries was held in Belgrade.

Liberation of Goa, Daman and Diu (1961)

- In December 1961, as a part of Operation Vijay, Indian armed forces launched a land, sea and air attack on Goa.
- The liberation of Goa and Daman & Diu took place on December 19, 1961. Before the invasion of these places by Indian forces happened, both the areas belonged to Portuguese India. Notably, the Portuguese ruled these colonies for over 450 years.
- A decade-and-half later, in 1975, India integrated Sikkim into the Union.

Sino-India War (1962)

- On October 20, 1962, China invaded India in both the eastern and the western theatre
- The trigger for the war between India and China was a border issue, with the Chinese side refusing to accept the McMohan Line and Line of Actual Control.
- The war ended with China declaring a ceasefire in a month.
- China's annexation of Tibet and the Dalai Lama's decision to flee to India created an atmosphere of distrust.

Jawaharlal Nehru dies (1964)

- On May 27, 1964, Jawaharlal Nehru died. But Nehru had brought back Lal Bahadur Shastri, a low-key Congress stalwart, as minister.

The Second India-Pakistan War (1965)

- Pakistan launched Operation Gibraltar in August 1965.
- The plan was to covertly send Pakistani army personnel, commence a guerrilla war, destroy infrastructure, attack Indian presence — and bank on local participation.
- The plan failed. Kashmiris did not back Pakistan, India learnt of the infiltration and began its counter-attack, opening up a front in Pakistan's Punjab, with troops inching towards Lahore.
- Eventually, a ceasefire was declared in late September.
- The ceasefire was followed by the Tashkent Declaration, mediated by Soviet Union
- PM Lal Bahadur Shastri died soon after signing the pact in January 1966.

Arrival of Indira Gandhi (1966)

- Indira Gandhi, the daughter of Jawaharlal Nehru, defeated Morarji Desai in party elections to succeed Shastri as PM

Weakening of Congress (1967)

- In 1962, the party won 361 seats with a 44% vote share in the Lok Sabha. In 1967, it won 283 seats with a 40% vote share.

- While the Dravida Munnetra Kazgham came to power in Madras, the communists led by EMS Namboodiripad returned to power in Kerala.

- Bengal saw the formation of a non-Congress government led by a Congress breakaway group, but with substantial Left presence.

- In UP and Bihar, the opposition, from socialists of various hues to the Bharatiya Jana Sangh, united to oust the Congress.

- These coalitions often didn't last, but they made it possible to imagine a political life outside of Congress hegemony.

The Congress Split (1969)

- One of the defining moments of Indira Gandhi's tenure was the split of the Indian National Congress into two factions in 1969.

- On one side was the 'Syndicate', a group of powerful regional party leaders - Congress (O)

- On the other side was Indira Gandhi and her supporters- Congress(R) or Congress (I)' (for Indira).

- The split significantly altered the political landscape of India, with Indira Gandhi's 'Congress (I)' eventually emerging as the dominant faction.

Bank nationalisation (1969)

- Fourteen banks were nationalised by the government on July 19, 1969.

- The second wave of nationalisation in banking came into effect on April 1980.

White Revolution (1970)

- In 1970, India saw the White Revolution (Operation Flood) — the world's biggest dairy development program, pioneered by Verghese Kurien.

- It transformed India from a milk deficient nation into the world's largest milk producer.

Liberation of Bangladesh (1971)

- India and Pakistan fight another major war over East Pakistan which ends after 90,000 Pakistani troops surrender and leads to the creation of Bangladesh

- East Pakistanis fought for independence from Pakistan and achieved it on March 26, 1971, under the leadership of Sheikh Mujibur Rahman.

Simla Agreement (1972)

- India and Pakistan signed the pact in 1972 "to settle their differences by peaceful means through bilateral negotiations".

Basic structure doctrine is articulated (1973)

- In the landmark 1973 *Kesavananda Bharati versus the State of Kerala* case, the Supreme Court articulated its basic structure doctrine.

- It recognised that the legislature did have the power to amend and that fundamental rights could be bridged — but there could be no amendment, no change, that violated the basic structure of the Indian Constitution both in terms of its principles and structure.

Chipko Movement (1973)

- The Chipko Andolan was a forest conservation movement in India. It began in 1973 in Reni village of Chamoli district, Uttarakhand.

Pokhran 1(1974)

- India conducted its first nuclear test, codenamed "Smiling Buddha", in the year 1974.
- With this, India broke into the list of five nuclear-powered nations.

JP Movement (1974)

- JP launches total revolution
- It was a movement initiated by students in Bihar against misrule and corruption. It was led by socialist Jayaprakash Narayan.
- The chain of events which JP set in motion through his clarion call would lead to the imposition of Emergency in India and, two years later, the election of first non-Congress government at the centre.

First Indian satellite made (1975)

- India designed first space satellite in 1975, named it after astronomer Aryabhata.

Sikkim became the 22nd State of the Indian Union (1975)

- The kingdom (Chogyal, Sikkim's monarch) opted to become full-fledged State of the Indian Union with effect from 26 April, 1975 vide the Constitution 36th Amendment Act 1975 with special provision laid for the State under article 371(F) of the Constitution of India.

Emergency (1975-1977)

- On June 25, 1975, India began the darkest political chapter in its post-independence history when Prime Minister Indira Gandhi imposed internal emergency in the country.
- Due to prevailing "internal tensions", then prime minister Indira Gandhi declared a state of Emergency that lasted from 1975 to 1977.
- It resulted in the suspension of elections and curbing of civil liberties.

42nd amendment (1976)

- This amendment was passed by parliament on November 11, 1976, during the emergency.
- Almost all the changes the 42nd amendment introduced to the constitution were aimed at tilting the balance of power towards the executive at the level of the centre, both vis-à-vis the judiciary and the state governments.
- This included annulling the spirit of the *Kesavananda Bharti judgment* which said that the parliament could not make changes to the basic structure of the constitution and shifting powers from the states to the centre.
- Secular and socialist were added to the preamble of the constitution.

Mass sterilisation (1976)

- The campaign was initiated by Sanjay Gandhi and saw about 6.2 million men sterilised in a year

Morarji Desai becomes first non-Congress PM (1977)

- The Janata Party, a group of parties opposed to the Emergency, defeated the Congress in 1977 elections and Morarji Desai became the first non-Congress PM of independent India.

Daman and Diu received the status of Union territory (1978)

- Daman and Diu received the status of Union territory in 1978. Recently, the Union Territories (UTs) of Dadra and Nagar Haveli and Daman and Diu were merged into one UT by the Dadra and Nagar Haveli and Daman and Diu Merger Act, 2019.

Mandal Commission formed (1979)

- The Mandal Commission was set up in 1979 under BP Mandal to identify the socially and educationally backward classes of India.

Indira Gandhi back as PM (1980)

- January 1980 - Indira Gandhi wins back power, becomes PM.

India sends man into space (1984)

- India sent its first astronaut, Rakesh Sharma, into space in 1984 in a joint mission with the Soviet Union.

Operation Blue Star (1984)

- It was the codename for military action to remove militant leader Jarnail Singh Bhindranwale and his followers from the Golden Temple complex in Amritsar.

Indira Gandhi is assassinated (1984)

- On October 31, 1984 Prime Minister Indira Gandhi was shot dead by her two Sikh body guards.

Anti-Sikh riots (1984)

- The 1984 anti-Sikh massacre was a series of attacks against Sikhs after Indira Gandhi was assassinated by her Sikh bodyguards. The carnage left nearly 3,000 people dead.

India's youngest PM - Rajiv Gandhi (1984)

- Rajiv Gandhi marked India's largest mandate in 1984, soon after his mother Indira Gandhi's assassination, and the sudden rise to power of the country's youngest prime minister at just 40 years of age

Bhopal gas tragedy (1984)

- The Bhopal disaster was a gas leak incident on the night of December 3, 1984 at the Union Carbide India Limited pesticide plant in Bhopal, Madhya Pradesh that killed more than 3000 people and left thousands with disabilities.

Assam Accord signed (1985)

- The Assam Accord, a memorandum of settlement signed in 1985 between the Indian government and leaders of the anti-foreigners Assam Movement, was aimed at settling an agitation launched by the All Assam Students' Union (AASU) six years earlier. The bone of contention was alleged illegal migration from Bangladesh, particularly after its war of independence in 1971

Punjab Accord (1985)

- The Punjab Accord, also known as the Rajiv-Longowal Accord, was signed in July 1985 between Prime Minister Rajiv Gandhi and Akali Dal leader Harchand Singh Longowal.
- It was aimed at promoting peace and stability in the insurgency-ridden Punjab.

Shah Bano case(1985) and Ayodhya dispute (1986)

- The other long-term development during this period was the rise of politics based on religious identity
- After the fall of the Janata Party and its break- up, the supporters of erstwhile Jana Sangh formed the Bharatiya Janata Party (BJP) in 1980.
- The BJP pursued the politics of 'Hindutva' and adopted the strategy of mobilising the Hindus.
- Hindutva literally means 'Hinduness' and was defined by its originator, V. D. Savarkar, as the basis of Indian (in his language also Hindu) nationhood.
- It basically meant that to be members of the Indian nation, everyone must not only accept India as their 'fatherland' (pitrubhu) but also as their holy land (punyabhu).
- Two developments around 1986 became central to the politics of BJP as a 'Hindutva' party.

The first was the Shah Bano case in 1985.

- In this case a 62-year old divorced Muslim woman, had filed a case for maintenance from her former husband.
- The Supreme Court ruled in her favour.
- The orthodox Muslims saw the Supreme Court's order as an interference in Muslim Personal Law.
- On the demand of some Muslim leaders, the government passed the Muslim Women (Protection of Rights on Divorce) Act, 1986 that nullified the Supreme Court's judgment.
- This action of the government was opposed by many women's organisations, many Muslim groups and most of the intellectuals.
- The BJP criticised this action of the Congress government as an unnecessary concession and 'appeasement' of the minority community.

The second was the Ayodhya dispute

- The second development was the order by the Faizabad district court in February 1986.
- The court ordered that the Babri Masjid premises be unlocked so that Hindus could offer prayers at the site which they considered as a temple.
- A dispute had been going on for many decades over the mosque known as Babri Masjid at Ayodhya.

- The Babri Masjid was a 16th century mosque in Ayodhya and was built by Mir Baqi – Mughal emperor Babur's General.
- Some Hindus believe that it was built after demolishing a temple for Lord Rama in what is believed to be his birthplace.
- The dispute took the form of a court case and has continued for many decades.
- In the late 1940s the mosque was locked up as the matter was with the court.
- As soon as the locks of the Babri Masjid were opened, mobilisation began on both sides.
- This large scale mobilisation led to surcharged atmosphere and many instances of communal violence
- The BJP made this issue its major electoral and political plank.
- The BJP, in order to generate public support, took out a massive march called the Rathyatra from Somnath in Gujarat to Ayodhya in UP.

Bofors scandal (1986)

- The Bofors scandal was a major corruption case involving the purchase of howitzer guns between India and Sweden and is believed to be one of the reasons for the downfall of the Rajiv Gandhi government in 1989 elections.

Goa became a State of the Indian Union(1987)

- In 1987, Goa became a State of the Indian Union.

Bhagalpur riots (1989)

- The Bhagalpur riots of 1989 were one of the worst Hindu-Muslim violence in independent India at the time and violent incident continued for two months, leaving 1000 people dead and 50,000 displaced.

Bommai case (1989)

- The Supreme Court laid down legal principles for the lawful and valid exercise of the power under Article 356, while underscoring the federal structure and the roles of President and governor.
- Bommai's judgment laid down the supremacy of the floor test in determining the support enjoyed by the party in power.
- It held that Article 356 should be used sparingly, and never for political gain or to get rid of an inconvenient state government, adding its use is amenable to judicial review.
- The Bommai verdict prescribes important constitutional guarantees against the abuse of Article 356.

General Election 1989 (Era of Coalitions)

- Elections in 1989 - Congress was the largest party in the Lok Sabha but it did not have a clear majority
- The National Front (which itself was an alliance of Janata Dal and some other regional parties) received support from two diametrically opposite political groups: the BJP and the Left Front.
- On this basis, the National Front formed a coalition government, but the BJP and the Left Front did not join in this government.

What happened after 1989

- Emergence of several parties in such a way that one or two parties did not get most of the votes or seats.
- This also meant that no single party secured a clear majority of seats in any Lok Sabha election held since 1989 till 2014.
- This development initiated an era of coalition governments at the Centre, in which regional parties played a crucial role in forming ruling alliances.

Alliance politics

- The nineties also saw the emergence of powerful regional parties
- These parties played an important role in the United Front government that came to power in 1996.
- The United Front was similar to the National Front of 1989 for it included Janata Dal and several regional parties.
- This time the BJP did not support the government. The United Front government was supported by the Congress.
- In 1989, both the Left and the BJP supported the National Front Government because they wanted to keep the Congress out of power.
- In 1996, the Left continued to support the non- Congress government but this time the Congress, supported it, as both the Congress and the Left wanted to keep the BJP out of power.
- BJP emerged as the largest party in the 1996 election but could not secure a majority in the Lok Sabha.
- It finally came to power by leading It finally came to power by leading a coalition government from May 1998 to June 1999 and was re-elected in October 1999.
- Atal Behari Vajpayee was the Prime Minister during both these NDA governments and his government formed in 1999 completed its full term.
- Thus, with the elections of 1989, a long phase of coalition politics began in India.

Government formed with the participation or support of many regional parties.

1. National Front in 1989
2. United Front in 1996 and 1997
3. NDA in 1997
4. BJP-led coalition in 1998
5. NDA in 1999
6. UPA in 2004 and 2009.

This trend changed in 2014.

Political Rise of Other Backward Classes

- One long-term development of this period was the rise of backward Classes as a political force.
- OBC - These are communities other than SC and ST
- The rise of these parties first found political expression at the national level in the form of the Janata Party government in 1977.

- The decision of the National Front government to implement the recommendations of the Mandal Commission further helped in shaping the politics of 'Other Backward Classes'.
- In 1978 the Backward and Minority Communities Employees Federation (BAMCEF) was formed.
- It took a strong position in favour of political power to the 'bahujan' – the SC, ST, OBC and minorities.
- It was out of this that the subsequent Dalit Shoshit Samaj Sangharsh Samiti and later the Bahujan Samaj Party (BSP) emerged under the leadership of Kanshi Ram.
- The BSP began as a small party supported largely by Dalit voters in Punjab, Haryana and Uttar Pradesh.
- But in 1989 and the 1991 elections, it achieved a breakthrough in Uttar Pradesh.
- This was the first time in independent India that a political party supported mainly by Dalit voters had achieved this kind of political success.

Mandal agitation (1990)

- VP Singh government implemented the Mandal Commission's recommendations to give 27% reservations in jobs and education for Other Backward Classes.
- The whole country was in the grip of protests against giving government jobs to certain castes on the basis of birth.

About the History of Mandal Commission

- Reservations for the OBC were in existence in southern States since the 1960s
- But this policy was not operative in north Indian States.
- During the tenure of Janata Party government in 1977-79, the demand for reservations for backward castes in north India and at the national level was strongly raised.
- The central government appointed a Commission in 1978 to look into and recommend ways to improve the conditions of the backward classes.
- This was the second time since Independence that the government had appointed such a commission.
- Therefore, this commission was officially known as the Second Backward Classes Commission.
- Popularly, the commission is known as the Mandal Commission, after the name of its Chairperson, Bindeshwari Prasad Mandal.
- The Commission gave its recommendations in 1980. By then the Janata government had fallen.
- The Commission recommended reserving 27 per cent of seats in educational institutions and government jobs for these groups.
- The Mandal Commission also made many other recommendations, like, land reform, to improve the conditions of the OBCs.
- In August 1990, the National Front government decided to implement one of the recommendations of Mandal Commission
- This decision sparked agitations and violent protests in many cities of north India.
- The decision was also challenged in the Supreme Court and came to be known as the 'Indira Sawhney case', after the name of one of the petitioners.
- In November 1992, the Supreme Court gave a ruling upholding the decision of the government.

Kuwait airlift (1990)

- The 1990 airlift of Indians from Kuwait was carried out from August 13, 1990, to October 20, 1990, after the invasion of Kuwait. Air India helped evacuate nearly 175,000 people.

V.P. Singh's Government (1990)

- V.P. Singh became the Prime Minister and led a short-lived government marked by social and political
- Chandra Shekhar Azad succeeded Singh but served for a brief period.

Rajiv Gandhi assassinated (1991)

- Then prime minister Rajiv Gandhi was assassinated by the Liberation Tigers of Tamil while on a campaign trail at Sriperumbudur on May 21, 1991.
- The assassination of Rajiv Gandhi in May 1991 led to a change in leadership of the Congress party.
- He was assassinated by a Sri Lankan Tamil linked to the LTTE when he was on an election campaign tour in Tamil Nadu.
- In the elections of 1991, Congress emerged as the single largest party.
- Following Rajiv Gandhi's death, the party chose Narsimha Rao as the Prime Minister.

General Elections (1991)

- The decline of Congress dominance began after the 1989 elections, and it couldn't secure a clear majority in the 1991 elections following Rajiv Gandhi's assassination.
- The Congress formed a minority government under P.V. Narasimha Rao, which survived its full term through negotiation and compromise, marking the beginning of coalition politics at the centre.

P.V. Narasimha Rao's Government (1991)

- The Congress party, under the leadership of P.V. Narasimha Rao, returned to power after the 1991 general elections.
- The government introduced significant economic reforms, known as Liberalisation, Privatization, and Globalization (LPG), to revitalise the Indian economy.

Globalisation of economy (1991)

- On July 24, 1991, finance minister Manmohan Singh presented a Budget which would change the face of the Indian economy forever.
- Indian economy opened the doors for free trade by foreign investors.

Panchayati Raj System (1992)

- The 73rd Amendment brought the Panchayati Raj System to rural India; the 74th Amendment brought the Municipality system to urban India. The 73rd and 74th Amendments Act was passed in the year 1992.

Babri Masjid demolition (1992)

- On December 6, 1992, the disputed Babri Masjid at Ayodhya was demolished by Hindu nationalist groups leading to riots across India, Over 2,000 people were killed in the riots.

- The final judgement in the Ayodhya dispute was declared by the Supreme Court of India on 9 November 2019.The Supreme Court ordered the disputed land (2.77 acres) to be handed over to a trust (to be created by the government of India) to build the Ram Janmabhoomi (revered as the birthplace of Hindu deity, Rama) temple. The court also ordered the government to give an alternative 5 acres of land in another place to the Uttar Pradesh Sunni Central Waqf Board for the purpose of building a mosque as a replacement for the demolished Babri Masjid.

Securities scam (1992)

- The 1992 Securities Scam is one of the biggest scams in the history of India stock market and was perpetrated by a stockbroker named Harshad Mehta.

Mumbai blasts (1993)

- The 1993 Bombay blasts were a series of bombings coordinated by gangster Dawood Ibrahim.

Formation of BJP government (1998)

- The BJP formed its first government under Prime Minister Atal Bihari Vajpayee but it lasted for only a year. Following fresh polls, BJP came back to power, becoming the first non-Congress government to do so.

Pokhran II (1998)

- India conducted a series of five nuclear bomb tests at Pokhran, Rajasthan, in May 1998 under the codename "Operation Shakti". It led to India becoming a full-fledged nuclear state.

Kargil war (1999)

- India launched 'Operation Vijay' after Pakistani forces infiltrated inside LoC.
- The war ended in July, with India successfully recapturing Tiger Hill.

IC-814 hijack (1999)

- Indian Airlines flight IC-814, on its way back to Delhi from Kathmandu, on December 24, 1999, was taken over by five Pakistani hijackers with 180 passengers and crew on board. They were released in exchange of three terrorists held by India.

Lahore declaration (1999)

- In a bid to quell the tensions, India and Pakistan signed the Lahore Declaration in February 1999 to avoid unauthorised operational use of nuclear weapons.

Creation of new states (2000)

- The new states of Chhattisgarh, Uttarakhand, and Jharkhand were formed on the 1st, 9th, and 15th of November 2000, respectively. It changed the count of Indian states from 25 to 28.

Golden Quadrilateral project (2001)

- In 2001, the Vajpayee govt launched the Golden Quadrilateral, the largest highway project in India connecting four major cities of Delhi, Mumbai, Chennai, and Kolkata.

Parliament attack (2001)

- Terrorist attack on the Parliament of India in New Delhi.

Gujarat riots(2002)

- The burning of a train in Godhra on February 27, 2002, triggered one of the worst communal riots in the history of India.

Right to Information Act (2005)

- The RTI Act was passed by Parliament in 2005, throwing government departments open to scrutiny and helping people to acquire any information they want from government officials.

MGNREGA Act (2005)

- Mahatma Gandhi National Rural Development Act, which is the largest work guarantee programme in the world, was enacted in 2005 with the primary objective of guaranteeing 100 days of wage employment per year to rural households.

Reopening Nathu La (2006)

- The mountain pass in the Himalayas that connects Sikkim and Tibet is one of the three open trading border posts between China and India. It was sealed by India after the 1962 Sino-Indian War. The pass was reopened in 2006.

1st Women President of India (2007)

- Pratibha Patil becomes the first woman President of India.

Chandrayaan 1 (2008)

- India successfully launched Chandrayaan in October 2008 to explore the moon. One of the greatest achievements of Chandrayaan was the discovery of water molecules in the lunar soil.

Mumbai terror attacks (2008)

- Pakistan-based terror outfit Lashkar-e-Taiba carried out a series of terrorist attacks in Mumbai in November 2008, leaving 166 people dead.

Right to Education Act (2009)

- Parliament passed the RTE Bill in 2009, making education a fundamental right of every child and bridged the gap between different classes of society. It requires all private schools to reserve 25 per cent seats for poor children.

First indigenous nuclear submarine launched (2009)

- India launched INS Arihant, the country's first indigenous nuclear submarine armed with ballistic missiles with a range of 3,500 km.

Commonwealth Games (2010)

- India hosted the 2010 Common Wealth Games in Delhi

Lokpal agitation (2011)

- Spearheaded by activist Anna Hazare, India Against Corruption movement that began in 2011 was a series of protests held across India for a Jan Lokpal bill to check graft in politics. The bill was finally passed by Parliament in 2013.

National Food Security Act (2013)

- The National Food Security Act, 2013 (also Right to Food Act), which aims to provide subsidised food grains to approximately two-thirds of India's 1.2 billion people, was signed into law on September 12, 2013.

Mars Orbiter Mission (2013)

- On November 5, 2013, Indian Space Research Organisation successfully launched Mars Orbiter Mission to probe Mars. It is the first Asian nation to reach Mars orbit, and the first nation in the world to do so in its first attempt.
- On November 5, 2013, Indian Space Research Organisation successfully launched Mars Orbiter Mission to probe Mars.

India launches its own GPS system (2013)

- India successfully launched NAVIC (Navigation with Indian Constellation), an independent regional navigation satellite system on par with US-based GPS.

Polio eradication (2014)

- In March 2014, the World Health Organisation certified the South-East Asian region – which includes India, a polio-free region.
  Other diseases like plague, leprosy, and smallpox have been declared eradicated from India.

Telangana statehood (2014)

- On June 2, 2014, Telangana was separated from the northwestern part of Andhra Pradesh as the newly formed 29th state with Hyderabad as its permanent capital.

Barack Obama attended India's Republic Day parade (2015)

- US President Barack Obama becoming the first US head of state to attend India's Republic Day parade.

Surgical Strike (2016)

- First surgical strike against Pakistan across the Line of Control in Pakistani-administered Kashmir.

Demonetisation (2016)

- In 2016, the government announced the demonetisation of Rs 500 and Rs 1,000 banknotes.

Goods and Services Tax (2017)

- GST (Goods and Services Tax) is one indirect tax for the whole nation and became effective from July 1, 2017.
- It is the resultant tax after subsuming major central and state taxes.

SC strikes down triple talaq (2017)

- The Supreme Court struck down the practice of instant triple talaq or talaq-e-biddat in which Muslim men divorce their wives by uttering talaq three times in quick succession.

SC decriminalises homosexuality(2018)

- The Supreme Court restored a landmark Delhi High Court judgment in 2018 that decriminalised homosexuality.

Tejas gets nod clearance to be inducted in IAF (2019)

- In February 2019, India's first indigenously developed light combat aircraft Tejas received the final operational clearance for induction into IAF.

Mission Shakti (2019)

- On March 27, 2019, India successfully conducted Mission Shakti – an anti-satellite missile test that could destroy satellites in space through missiles on the ground.

Chnadrayaan 2 (2019)

- Chandrayaan-2 is the second lunar exploration mission developed by the Indian Space Research Organisation, after Chandrayaan-1
- It consists of a lunar orbiter, a lander, and the Pragyan rover, all of which were developed in India

Revocation of Article 370 and 35A (2019)

- On August 5, 2019, the President of India revoked the special status of J&K, effectively nullifying Article 370 and Article 35A.
- The Jammu and Kashmir Reorganisation Act, 2019 was passed by the Parliament, dividing J&K into two Union Territories: Jammu and Kashmir, and Ladakh.

Chandrayaan-3 (2023)

- It is a planned third lunar exploration mission by the Indian Space Research Organisation (ISRO).
- It will consist of a lander and a rover similar to Chandrayaan-2, but would not have an orbiter. Its propulsion module will behave like a communication relay satellite.
- The propulsion module will carry the lander and rover configuration until the spacecraft is in a 100 km lunar orbit.
- Chandrayaan 3 propulsion module, which will be used as a relay satellite
- Following Chandrayaan-2, where a last-minute software glitch in the soft landing guidance software led to the failure of the lander's soft landing attempt after a successful orbital insertion, another lunar mission was proposed.
- The launch of Chandrayaan-3 has been scheduled for July 14, 2023